Café Max & Rosie's

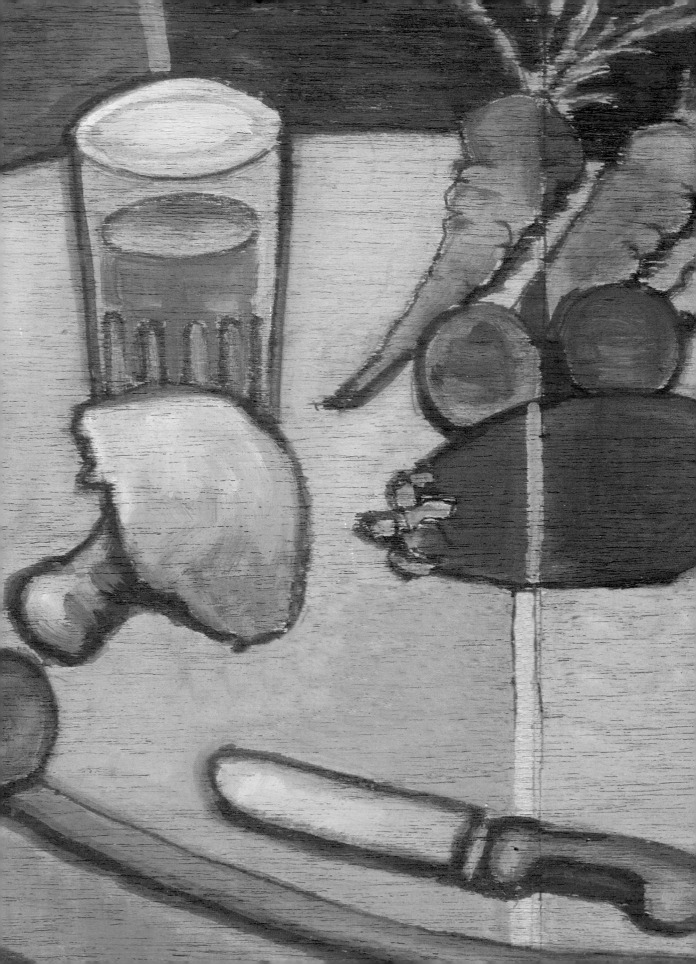

Café Max & Rosie's

Vegetarian Cooking with Health and Spirit

by Max and Rosie Beeby

TEN SPEED PRESS
Berkeley • Toronto

A Kirsty Melville Book

Ten Speed Press
PO Box 7123
Berkeley, California 94707
www.tenspeed.com

Distributed in Australia by Simon & Schuster Australia, in Canada by Ten Speed Press
Canada, in New Zealand by Southern Publishers Group, in South Africa by Real Books,
in Southeast Asia by Berkeley Books, and in the United Kingdom and Europe by Airlift
Book Company.

Cover design by Jeffery Puda
Text design by Nancy Austin
Illustrations by Max Beeby

Library of Congress Cataloging-in-Publication Data
Beeby, Max.
  Café Max & Rosie's : vegetarian cooking with health and spirit / by Max & Rosie Beeby.
    p. cm.
  ISBN 1-58008-237-8
   1. Vegetarian cookery. 2. Vegetable juices. 3. Fruit juices. 4. Café Max & Rosie's.
I. Title: Café Max and Rosie's. II. Beeby, Rosie. III. Title.

TX837 .B39 2000
641.5'636—dc21

                                                                00-060757

Printed in Hong Kong
First printing, 2000

This book is dedicated to our loyal customers.

Contents

Café Max & Rosie's

vi

PART II: JUST JUICE IT!

Café Max & Rosie's

Preface

Most people forget that food is one of the most important things in life. It provides nourishment to sustain a strong, healthy body and mind, and is a major factor in determining the quality of our lives. The connection between food and health is common sense. What's the benefit of owning everything in the world if you have poor health?

Before the 1950s life did not include fast foods, processed foods, chemicals, or preservatives, and fatal diseases (such as cancer and heart disease) were not as prevalent as they are today. People who take the time to feed themselves and their families with love and care contribute greatly to their physical, mental, social, and spiritual health.

Café Max & Rosie's is not just another vegetarian café—it's a way of life. We have been feeding local Ashevillians and visitors healthy foods since 1992. The café is, for us, an outreach for right livelihood. It may surprise you to know that in our little southern town, we have now served more than 80,000 veggie burgers. Move over McWho?! We like to think that our small gesture of serving healthy food is helping to move our planet in the right direction.

We have an old saying at the café, "Give a person tofu and they may not eat it. Teach a person to cook tofu, and you've created a vegetarian." Using simple and direct cooking instructions distilled from more than 15 years of teaching, Rosie has created hundreds of vegetarians during her evening cooking classes, offered in a series three times a year at the café. People from all walks of life come together to learn Rosie's unique cooking style, and in the chapters that follow we'll walk you through Rosie's classes, step by simple step.

While inexperienced cooks may be a little timid at first, we've found that no one can resist the casual atmosphere of learning that produces such delicious foods full of love. In the simple act of coming together and cooking food, a wonderful communion happens. No matter what types of people have taken Rosie's classes, the transformation is always the same. Becoming a vegetarian does not mean being deprived of good-tasting food, it means stepping strongly in the direction of good health. We're thrilled to be able to share the lessons learned in Rosie's classes with a wider audience. The time is right.

To assist newcomers with creating complete vegetarian meals, we've included a menu at the end of each chapter highlighting a main dish from that chapter, and using side dishes from other chapters to round out the meal. In some cases the menu includes very simple accompaniments (like steamed asparagus or a fresh baguette) for which there are no recipes in this book. We have, however, given simple directions for preparing these accompaniments (if necessary) in the menu introduction.

Throughout the years we've been blessed with a colorful and enthusiastic group of employees. Because we've come to consider these coworkers part of our family, we knew this cookbook wouldn't be complete without their voices. So we asked a few current and former employees to contribute stories about their time at the café, and we collected our memories of them in response. These personal anecdotes appear in each chapter. We hope they give you some idea of what a lively little place Café Max & Rosie's can be.

Although the juice bar was not part of the original Café Max & Rosie's, the popularity of our smoothies has grown by leaps and bounds over the past few years. The demand for freshly squeezed juices is on the rise because besides tasting delicious, their health benefits are becoming more widely known. Our recipes are simple, refreshing, delicious, and healthful.

When you walk through the door at Café Max & Rosie's, your senses are bombarded by delicious smells escaping from the kitchen, sweet music being played on the grand piano, and bursts of

vibrant color from Max's original artwork hanging on the walls. Lush green plants, hanging fruits and vegetables, and watermelon tablecloths add to the unique look of the café and contribute to the friendly and intimate environment that makes this place special. As you browse through the pages of our first cookbook, we hope that the combination of Max's art, Rosie's recipes, and stories from the café let you experience a tiny bit of what Café Max & Rosie's is all about.

We hope you will enjoy preparing our dishes as much as we enjoy serving them at the café. Partaking of tasty vegetarian food is a good first step on the evolutionary ladder to vegetarianism. We at Café Max & Rosie's are here to facilitate that transformation by serving thousands of healthy, nourishing meals every year. The thanks we get from customers for being here, the many requests we get to open Café Max & Rosie's in various cities worldwide, the many people who have never liked tofu until they've had Rosie's (including Max!)— these are the rewards of owning a vegetarian café. Since Day One our customers have been asking for our recipes, and our reply has always been the same: All will be revealed in our cookbook. This book is a fulfillment of the many thousands of promises we have made. Passing these recipes on to you is an honor.

May you make use of this book in good health. Let the cooking begin....

Acknowledgments

To Rosina and Erni, Max's Mom and Dad, and Sol and Eddi, Rosie's Mom and Dad. We thank you for the many blessings we have received from you.

To the people who have made Café Max & Rosie's possible. First, all thanks to David Brown, our landlord. There can be no higher praise than to say he is a thorough gentleman. Next, to Larry and Martha and Janet and Evan, who were our dear friends when we were in need. They are true friends indeed.

To Rob Friedman, a great friend, musician, and songwriter. Also not bad with a brush. He helped paint the café pink when we first opened.

To Swami Virato, a good friend who has taught us so much about the art of friendship.

To Sol and Jeff. Their help has been invaluable and has truly made the café a family business.

To Dana, Mason, and Joshua, those incredible children whose hearty vegetarian appetites have helped in our success. They have all worked at the café, including Joshua, our eight-year-old. The thought of Josh standing on a stool washing dishes will always bring a smile to our faces.

To Margaret, for all her help with those incredible children.

To George, our wonderfully eccentric agent, for seeing the potential in our book.

To Ten Speed Press, a wonderful group of people, not quite how you imagine publishers to be. It's been a real pleasure to work with you all.

For inspiration, we would like to thank Paul and Linda McCartney, who have displayed their intelligence and good work through their efforts in the vegetarian lifestyle. May their positive presence be in the world for many generations to come.

To John Robbins, a sincere thank you for your forthright and intelligent observations on some of the follies of our times.

From Max: I wish to thank my four sisters, Doris, Auriol, Carole, and Lynda. I was indeed a thorn between four roses. I would also like to thank God for the blessing of meeting Fazal Inayat Khan, perhaps the most creative person I have ever met.

From Rosie: I would like to thank Lino Stanchich and Michio and Aveline Kushi for teaching me my beginnings in macrobiotic cooking, which led to a lifestyle change both in food and thought.

We would both like to thank our wonderful staff and our customers for making and keeping Max & Rosie's such a wonderfully different café.

The Ten Commandments
(Vegetarian, Naturally)

1. Thou shalt not eat animals.

2. Thou shalt not eat irradiated foods.

3. Thou shalt not eat genetically engineered foods—the same
    "rent-a-scientists" who told you that cigarette smoking
    was good for you are at it again.

4. Thou shalt not eat fast foods.

5. Thou shalt not eat fish. It is your foremost supplier of
    mercury, lead, dioxins, etc.

6. Thou shalt demand organically grown foods. (It is really
    hard to imagine there is another kind.)

7. Thou shalt honor the cook by paying attention when eating.

8. A blessing before eating is the spice that completes
    wholesome food.

9. What you do does matter.

10. Remember, being a vegetarian is the most powerful
    act an individual can do for the evolution of the planet.

Part I:
Rosie's Cooking Classes

An Introduction to Rosie's Kitchen

There are so many things to say when teaching people how to cook, it's difficult to know where to start. But, like running a café, at some point you just have to open the door, so here goes....

My cooking style is simple. I emphasize the natural flavors of foods rather than using a zillion herbs, spices, condiments, and sauces. Although each "class" has many recipes, I've tried to keep them simple so as not to overwhelm or confuse anyone. I have looked at recipes myself that required an hour's shopping for ingredients before even starting to cook! That's definitely not for me.

Cooking is an art, and like in any of the arts, you need to let your creativity flow and develop your own style. Initially, you may want to follow recipes exclusively, but a life of cooking only by following recipes makes for a dull cook. Believe me, cooking is not only fun, it's a joy; and creating your own dishes, or even making changes in recipes to better suit you, is something to take pride in. As the cook, you are providing your own as well as your family's nourishment, contributing to their good health at each meal. What I've realized while writing this book is that it is very easy for me to create dishes, but very difficult to write them down in recipes with measurements because I rarely measure! That's the freedom you want to have to make cooking a fun, creative process.

When planning your meals, try to think visually, especially with colors of foods. We are so lucky to have such a wide range of vegetables available to us, and the colors vary as much as the flavors. Using different color combinations allows for more variety, which is important nutritionally as well as visually. For example, putting a mound of plain brown rice, black beans, and steamed broccoli on a plate is a good enough meal, but it's not that appealing to the eye. By adding steamed carrots to the broccoli, onion and corn to

the black beans, and a scallion garnish with a sprinkle of sesame seeds to the rice, you still keep the meal extremely simple, but the presentation is a lot more appealing and the nutritional value greater.

When creating meals, you need to know what makes a nutritionally complete meal so that you are eating for optimal health. A complete meal consists of whole grains, lots of fresh vegetables, both cooked and raw, and a small amount of protein (soy products, beans, nuts, and seeds). Fresh fruits, either raw or cooked, are great between-meal snacks. Granted, not every meal I prepare sticks to these exact guidelines, but they're usually pretty close. A variety of vegetables provides an invaluable assortment of nutrients, especially when your meal includes different vegetables in the soup, the main dish, and the salad. Even a sandwich for lunch can be a complete meal, containing whole-grain bread, protein, and vegetables.

As you cook your way through the four basic cooking classes, you will learn to cook with beans, whole grains, soy (tofu and tempeh), and pasta. As you try new recipes, try to coordinate your cooking so that all the dishes are ready, for the most part, at the same time. For example, beans take the most time to cook, so start with them. While the beans are cooking, begin preparing other dishes that don't take quite as long. There are always vegetables to prep, even if you don't cook them until the very end. This really does take some coordination, as well as concentration; but as with anything else, the more you do it, the easier it becomes. Before long you'll be able to put meals together without a second thought.

To maintain a true vegetarian diet, processed foods, sugars, and animal products (including dairy products) should be avoided as much as possible. The quality of these foods is just not acceptable for human consumption. It makes sense, after all, that cow's milk is mother's milk for calves, not human babies, children, or adults. As a matter of fact, human beings are the only animals to consume milk past childhood. Your body always knows what is best for it; so if you tune into how different foods make you feel, you'll know what is best for you to eat.

ROSIE'S COOKING TIPS

Try to use organic, locally grown foods, and adjust your cooking to the seasons. Because we live in North Carolina, it is quite unnatural for us to eat grapes or strawberries in the winter as these fruits grow here naturally in the summer. They are either imported or transported long distances to get here, and lose a great deal of nutritional value and flavor along the way. Although in the U.S. we are spoiled with a great variety of fruits and vegetables year-round, try to recognize what is actually growing locally during whatever the season is, and use more of these fresh vegetables and fruits. Your health will benefit. A helpful tip for selecting fresh vegetables is by color. The more vibrant the colors, the better the quality.

Although I don't say it in the recipes, all vegetables must be washed before using. Wash root vegetables, such as carrots and potatoes, with a vegetable brush. We use organic vegetables so I'm not in the habit of peeling them; but if they are not organic, you may want to peel them as well.

In many recipes the vegetables are sautéed. To sauté means to cook food over high heat while stirring frequently so that the food cooks quickly and remains a bit crunchy. In most of my recipes I sauté in 1 to 2 tablespoons of oil only, as most vegetables have a high water content and give off liquid as they cook. You can always add more oil if necessary. Remember, before sautéing any foods, make sure the oil is hot; the hotter the oil, the less oil is absorbed by the food.

If you are especially concerned about your oil consumption, you can "water sauté." To water sauté you merely use water in place of the oil. It's almost like steaming, but you get more of a stir-fry flavor and consistency.

For some of the recipes I say to "quick sauté." This means to sauté the vegetables for only 1 to 2 minutes on high heat, as they will continue to cook as other ingredients are added. The purpose of a quick sauté is to enhance as well as seal in the flavor.

All vegetable oils have a distinctly different flavor, and you can change the taste of a dish simply by changing the oil you use. For the recipes that use olive oil, I prefer extra virgin, because the difference in flavor between extra virgin and pure olive oil is dramatic. I also use light sesame oil, toasted sesame oil, canola oil, safflower oil, and occasionally peanut oil.

Most of my recipes call for sea salt (which contains more minerals than ordinary table salt) and freshly ground black pepper. I don't state an amount because I believe everyone should decide for themselves how much seasoning to use. I do recommend, however, that you taste the dish before adding either, as it may not need any at all.

I use nutritional yeast in quite a few recipes. It is a wonderful food, high in B-complex vitamins. Its cheesy flavor complements pastas and salad dressings, and it's great on popcorn! My family is hooked on it, and what a great thing to be hooked on. You can find nutritional yeast at most health food stores.

Umeboshi vinegar is a Japanese plum vinegar made from umeboshi plums. It has a fruity tartness unlike other vinegars. I use it sparingly in salad dressings and sauces because it is a bit salty. You can find it at most health food stores or Asian markets.

I also use a cholesterol-free tofu mayonnaise in some dressings and on some of the sandwiches. Nayonnaise is the brand I prefer; it has a similar flavor and texture to mayonnaise.

I use tahini in many of my dressings, dips, and sauces. Tahini is a sesame butter not unlike peanut butter, but with a stronger flavor. It is high in protein and calcium, and is often used in Middle Eastern dishes.

Seitan, also known as wheat meat, is a high-protein food made from the gluten portion of wheat. I prefer Lightlife Savory Seitan, marinated in teriyaki sauce, which adds a nice flavor to any dish. You can make seitan yourself, if you have a lot of time and patience.

Quite a few of the recipes call for freshly squeezed ginger juice. You will need a ginger grater for this. It is very fine and has no holes. It merely grates the ginger into pulp right on the grater. You then squeeze the pulp in your hand to extract the juice into a measuring spoon.

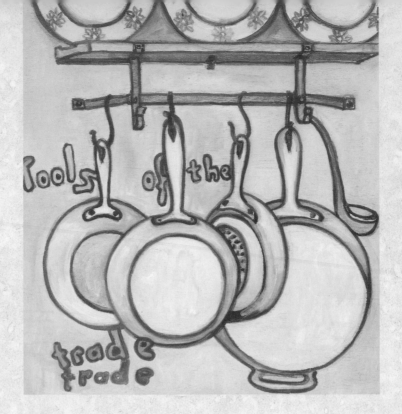

Tools of the trade trade

I do use feta cheese in a few of the recipes. Although it is a dairy product, it is a goat cheese, which is lower in fat and easier to digest than cow's milk cheese. I use it rarely; but in the recipes it appears in, it does add a nice flavor.

And finally, a small warning. I love fresh garlic. I use a lot of it in my recipes. I know garlic is not for everyone, so if you do not like it, use less or none at all. Also, be aware that garlic cloves vary in size. I, of course, use large ones as much as possible.

If you can, try to keep some cooking staples on hand. Whole grains (brown rice, millet, oats), pastas, and dried or canned beans store well and are great to keep stocked in your pantry. Keep a few of your favorite spices around as well. You will have to fill in with fresh vegetables (which I buy every one or two days), but a well-stocked kitchen will give you a chance to create meals with what you have on hand. Max and I actually stocked up for Y2K, and what a blessing it has been. I now keep a fully stocked kitchen, and it feels great!

By the way, if you're going to be spending a lot of time in your kitchen, you really need to like it! Even if your kitchen is small—if it is organized, has good lighting (preferably with windows), and nice colors—you will find you enjoy cooking in it. Growing fresh herbs in small pots on the windowsills does wonders. To me, the kitchen is the most important room in the house, and it has taken me a long time to get a good kitchen. Is it my ideal kitchen? No. But it definitely works and I like it. So do the best you can with what you have.

Here is a list of essential kitchen equipment:

- A GOOD CUTTING KNIFE. You may have to try some out before buying. (Kitchen stores will usually let you try out knives, although they tend be more expensive. Family and friends are good sources for testing cutlery, too.) I've used a Japanese Caddie brand knife for fifteen years that cost about $18.00 at the time I bought it. It doesn't have to be big or expensive, just use a size you're comfortable with.

- STAINLESS STEEL POTS WITH LIDS. The thicker and heavier the better, as they tend not to burn food as easily as thin pots and they distribute the heat more evenly. You will also want a vegetable steamer or basket to place in a pot for steaming vegetables. Please avoid aluminum pots, especially for boiling water, because over time, the aluminum is leached out and ingested.

- CAST-IRON SKILLETS. I use cast-iron exclusively for sautéing, as you can use a lot less oil than with stainless steel, and you actually get a slightly different flavor in the food. I have a medium (10-inch) and a large (13-inch) skillet that I use religiously. They are relatively inexpensive and must be treated with oil before initial use. To treat cast-iron pans, put a light coat of vegetable oil on all parts of the pan, both inside and out. Place it in a warm oven (250°) for about an hour. To maintain the pan, do not soak it in water, merely wipe it with a clean cloth (or use a wet sponge, but dry the pan immediately).

- CUTTING BOARD. I have a large wood cutting board but plastic works just as well. Make sure you get the size to suit you.

- UTENSILS. You will need spoons, preferably wooden, for stirring and mixing, plus a whisk, a wooden or metal spatula, a soup ladle, serving spoons, garlic press, pasta tongs, colander, vegetable peeler, vegetable brush, measuring cups and spoons, and a ginger grater (see page 5).

- ■ SMALL APPLIANCES. A blender, food processor, and toaster are definitely handy in the kitchen. You can live without the food processor, but it does work much better than a blender in many recipes.

An ideal kitchen would also have:

- ■ A GAS STOVE. Gas burners are much easier to cook on than electric burners, because you can adjust the temperature much faster and more accurately. Personally, I can't cook on anything else.

- ■ SPRING WATER. If you're not lucky enough to have your own spring water, I suggest you look into a good filtration system or buy bottled water.

- ■ LOTS OF COUNTER SPACE. Enough said.

All the recipes yield 4 to 6 servings (except the juice drinks, which yield one 10-ounce or 16-ounce serving); however, I based the yields on my family, who are known to consume some pretty hefty portions of food. Your servings may be a bit different than what is stated. Also, be aware that some of the recipes are the main dish of the meal, whereas others are side dishes and therefore not meant to make as much as a main course.

The sequence of the cooking classes is relevant, so I recommend that you work your way through them in the order in which they appear. Cooking instructions come with each class, and you will need to understand the material in the first class in order to make the recipes in later classes. If you don't have time to do all the classes in order, the cooking instructions are carefully cross-referenced, so you should be able to open the book to any recipe and prepare it successfully.

By the way, a timer comes in handy, and I strongly recommend that you clean as you go, or you'll have quite a cleanup after your meal.

Since each class involves a good amount of cooking, I don't recommend you set out by yourself to tackle an entire class in one sitting. You could make one or two recipes at a time, or get a group together and see what happens! Be sure to read through the recipes in each class before beginning, and most importantly, have fun!

Class 1: Beans

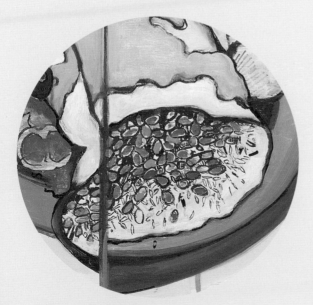

Beans

AN INTRODUCTION TO BEANS

Beans come in quite a variety of flavors and, with the help of spices and sauces, make delicious dishes to complete meals. When serving beans, always serve them with whole grains, and serve a small amount in comparison to the other foods of the meal.

As with whole grains, there is a wide variety of beans available to us, such as adzuki, Anasazi, black beans, garbanzo beans, Great Northern beans, kidney beans, lentils, lima beans, navy beans, pinto beans, and soybeans. Beans are high in protein and soluble fiber and are a great source of vitamins A, C, and B-complex; calcium; folic acid; and iron.

Most beans must be soaked before cooking, with a few exceptions. For beans that do not require soaking, make sure to rinse them before cooking. In general, soak dried beans for 6 to 8 hours. Discard the soaking water and rinse the beans before cooking. Use about 3 to 4 cups of water to cook 1 cup of dried beans (see Bean Cooking Chart). Place the rinsed beans, water, and a strip of kombu (a sea vegetable that aids in the digestion of beans) in a stainless steel pot, cover, and bring to a boil. If any foam rises to the top, skim it off with a large slotted spoon and discard it. Turn the heat very low, so that the water is just slightly bubbling, and simmer, covered, for the time specified in the Bean Cooking Chart. Don't add salt until the beans are soft, as it hardens their skins and interferes with the cooking process. After cooking beans for a couple of hours, the last thing you need is for them to be hard! Add about $1/8$ teaspoon sea salt per cup of dried beans.

Beans are fully cooked when they are soft and most or all of the water is absorbed. The Bean Cooking Chart gives cooking times but these may differ depending on the type of stove you use, the amount of beans you're cooking, and how many times you lift the lid to check them. So use the Bean Cooking Chart as a guide when checking the beans for doneness.

A very convenient way to cook beans is in a slow cooker. Beans can be soaked overnight, drained and rinsed, and brought to a boil on the stovetop. Then they can be transferred to a slow cooker set on

medium and cooked all day. Alternatively, you can soak them in the daytime and cook them overnight. But, beans for breakfast?

Because beans take so long to cook, I usually cook extra to use for other recipes during the week. They store well in the refrigerator for up to five days.

Aside from traditional American bean dishes, there are a great deal of ethnic ones, especially Mexican and Indian. Bean dips are great and easy to make, and leftover beans make great stews and burritos.

My advice for this class is to read over the recipes carefully and make sure to soak the beans as needed. It would be even better to cook the beans in advance. And if you do make more than one recipe at a time, I don't recommend you eat too many beans at once, especially if it's less than three hours before bedtime!

BEAN COOKING CHART

BEAN (1 cup dry)*	SOAKING TIME (hours)	WATER (cups)	COOKING TIME (hours)
Adzuki (azuki)	None	3	1-1$\frac{1}{2}$
Anasazi	6-8	3	1$\frac{1}{2}$
Black (turtle)	6-8	3	1$\frac{1}{2}$
Black-eyed peas	None	3	1
Garbanzos (chickpeas)	6-8	4	3
Fava (broad)	6-8	4	3
Great Northern	6-8	3	2
Kidney	6-8	3	1$\frac{1}{2}$
Lentil, green or red	None	3	45 minutes
Lima	6-8	3	1
Navy	6-8	3	1$\frac{1}{2}$
Pinto	6-8	3	2
Soybeans, yellow or black	8 or more	4	3-4
Split peas	None	2	45 minutes

*1 cup dry beans yields approximately 1$\frac{1}{2}$ to 2$\frac{1}{2}$ cups cooked beans.

Black Bean Chili

SERVES 4 TO 6

This is a great chili, chock-full of fresh vegetables. I like to serve it with corn-bread and salad. It can also be served over rice. If you don't like all the vegetables included in the recipe, leave them out or, preferably, substitute others.

2 cups dried black beans, soaked for 6 to 8 hours and drained

6 cups water

5 to 7 tablespoons extra virgin olive oil

1 large yellow onion, chopped

1 green bell pepper, seeded and coarsely chopped

1 red bell pepper, seeded and coarsely chopped

2 small zucchini, cubed

2 small yellow squash, cubed

2 plum tomatoes, chopped

4 cloves garlic, minced

1 small eggplant, cubed

2 cups fresh or frozen corn

1 (15-ounce) can tomato paste

1/4 cup freshly squeezed lime juice

2 teaspoons ground cumin

1/4 cup chili powder

1 tablespoon dried red pepper flakes

Sea salt and freshly ground black pepper

Fresh cilantro leaves for garnish

Combine the beans and water in a medium soup pot and cook according to the Bean Cooking Chart (see page 11).

Heat 2 to 3 tablespoons oil in a large cast-iron skillet over high heat. Add the onion, peppers, zucchini, yellow squash, tomatoes, and garlic and quick sauté for 2 to 3 minutes. Transfer to a large pot.

Heat the remaining 3 to 4 tablespoons oil in the skillet. When the oil is hot, add the eggplant and sauté for 5 to 8 minutes, or until the eggplant

begins to brown. Add the eggplant to the pot. Then add the corn, tomato paste, lime juice, cooked and drained beans, cumin, chili powder, and red pepper flakes.

Cook, covered, over low heat for approximately 30 minutes. Check periodically; if the chili is too dry, add some water. Add salt and pepper and adjust seasonings.

Serve garnished with fresh cilantro.

PAUL

Max & Rosie's always evokes good memories. Our association, though brief, had a strong impact on my life. Although I still think of myself as a fine sandwich maker, it must be admitted I am a better actor. When I am in town I always pop in to see my Max & Rosie's family. It is always great to be there. All the best with the book! Love, Paul

One late afternoon, a smiling, outgoing young man came through the door. He was Mr. Personality in the most agreeable way. He wanted a job. The next day he came to work looking like a model out of a fashion magazine. The day went on and he was charming, friendly, delightful—and useless at making sandwiches. What was clear was that Paul was management, not a worker! We parted company pleasantly. Max mentioned in passing that Paul should go into films. Paul still pops by to see us when he is not busy acting. How happy we are that his life is going well. (His real name has not been used to protect the innocent.)

Garbanzo Bean Stew with Eggplant and Tomato

SERVES 6 TO 8

This stew is a great winter dish. If you don't want to use any oil, you can skip the sautéing and just add the vegetables to the beans to cook. Of course, the oil does give it more flavor. I happen to like this stew with chopped red onion sprinkled on top. It's delicious over basmati rice. Remember to leave yourself enough time; garbanzo beans take a long time to cook.

1 1/2 cups dried garbanzo beans, soaked for 6 to 8 hours and drained

6 cups water

1 tablespoon mustard seeds

1 tablespoon turmeric

1 teaspoon ground cumin

2 teaspoons curry powder

2 tablespoons freshly squeezed ginger juice (see page 5)

1 cup coarsely chopped fresh cilantro

5 to 7 tablespoons extra virgin olive oil

1 red onion, chopped

2 large ripe tomatoes, chopped

2 pounds red potatoes, cut in 1-inch pieces

1 eggplant, cut in 1-inch pieces

Sea salt and freshly ground black pepper

Combine the beans, water, mustard seeds, turmeric, cumin, curry powder, ginger juice, and half the cilantro in a large soup pot. Cook according to the Bean Cooking Chart (see page 11).

About 1 1/2 hours after the beans have started cooking, heat 2 to 3 tablespoons of the oil in a large cast-iron skillet over high heat. Add the onion, tomatoes, and potatoes and quick sauté for 2 to 3 minutes. Transfer to the bean pot. Heat the remaining 3 to 4 tablespoons of oil in the skillet. When the oil is hot, add the eggplant and sauté for 5 to 8 minutes, or until the eggplant pieces begin to brown. Transfer the sautéed eggplant to the bean pot. Continue cooking for 1 1/2 hours, until the garbanzo beans are soft.

Season with salt and pepper and adjust the other seasonings, if necessary. Serve garnished with the remaining 1/2 cup of cilantro.

> *People often say that humans have always eaten animals,*
> *as if this is a justification for continuing the practice.*
> *According to this logic, we should not try to prevent*
> *people from murdering other people, since this has also*
> *been done since the earliest of times.* "
> —*Isaac Bashevis Singer*

Hummus

SERVES 4

I have eaten hummus in many places and have found each batch a bit different tasting. This is why I have written this recipe with such a range in ingredient amounts. You can see if you like more tahini or more lemon juice. And if you want more garlic, go for it! I recommend using a food processor for this recipe, as it does a better job of mixing than a blender. The hummus should be served chilled or at room temperature as a dip or sandwich spread.

1 1/2 cups dried garbanzo beans, soaked for 6 to 8 hours and drained

6 cups water

1/2 to 1 cup tahini

8 cloves garlic, pressed

1/4 to 1/2 cup freshly squeezed lemon juice

Sea salt and freshly ground black pepper

Combine the garbanzo beans and water and cook according to the Bean Cooking Chart (see page 11). Drain the beans and reserve the cooking water.

Combine the beans, tahini, garlic, and lemon juice in a food processor or blender and blend until smooth. If the mixture is too dry, add some of the reserved cooking liquid, a little at a time. Add salt and pepper and adjust the seasonings to taste. Serve immediately, or refrigerate for 30 minutes before serving.

Black Bean Burrito Ole!

SERVES 4

This recipe is perfect for using up leftover rice and black beans, or any other beans for that matter. So cook some extra beans for the Black Bean Chili (see page 12) and set them aside for this!

4 (10-inch) flour tortillas

4 cups cooked brown rice (see page 24)

4 cups cooked black beans, rinsed and drained (see page 11)

2 cups tightly packed chopped fresh spinach

2 to 3 cups crumbled feta cheese (optional but very tasty)

3 to 4 cups salsa

Sliced avocado for garnish

Black olives for garnish

Chopped leaf lettuce and tomato for garnish

Corn chips and Jericho Salsa (see page 130)

Lay the tortillas flat on a work surface. Divide the rice and beans into 4 equal portions and place a portion down the middle of each tortilla. Divide the spinach, feta cheese, and salsa into 4 equal portions and add to each tortilla. Fold the tortillas so the sides overlap. Turn them over and tuck the ends under.

Place the tortillas in a hot, lightly oiled, large cast-iron skillet. Cover, reduce the heat to medium, and cook for 5 minutes, until the tortillas are browned on one side.

Serve on individual plates and garnish with the avocado, black olives, lettuce, and tomato. Serve with corn chips and salsa on the side.

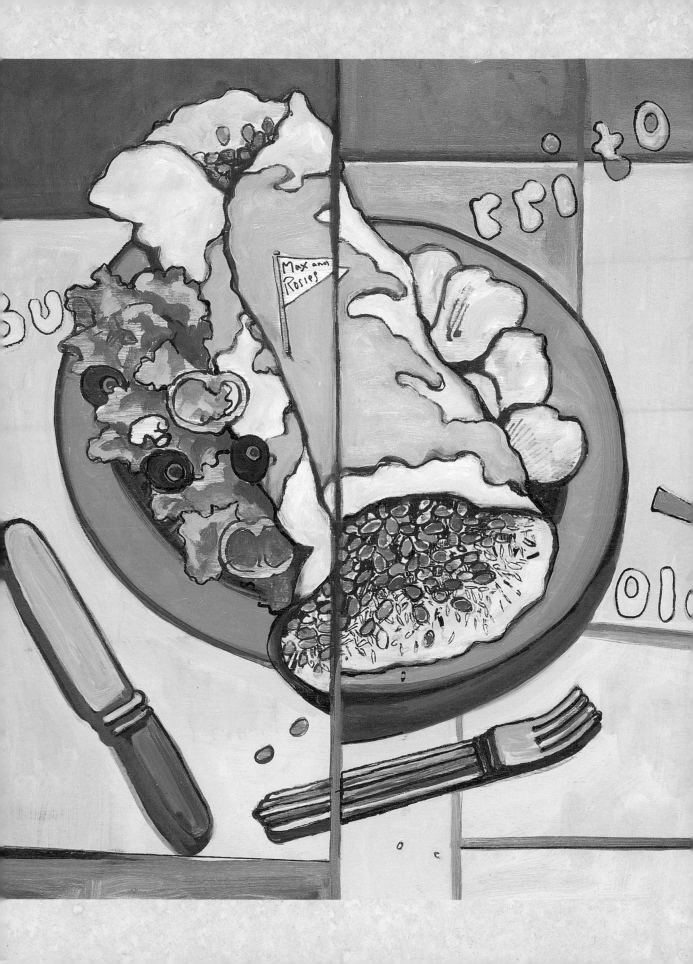

Italian-Style Kidney Beans

SERVES 4 TO 6

This is actually a very tasty risotto dish, using arborio rice, vegetables, and spices along with the beans. The consistency should be creamy. Try adding more vegetables, such as bell pepper, zucchini, or asparagus, for a change in the flavor.

1 cup dried kidney beans, soaked for 6 to 8 hours and drained

3 cups water

2 to 3 tablespoons extra virgin olive oil

4 cloves garlic, finely chopped

1 shallot, coarsely chopped

2 teaspoons dried oregano

1 1/2 cups arborio rice

1 cup fresh or frozen corn kernals

Pinch of cayenne pepper

Sea salt

3 1/2 to 4 cups vegetable stock (see page 67) or water

1 (6-ounce) can tomato paste

1/2 cup nutritional yeast

Freshly ground black pepper

Chopped fresh basil for garnish

Sliced black olives for garnish

Chopped red onion for garnish (optional)

" *The body is not fixed in time but a flowering event that must be nurtured.* "
—*Max*

Combine the kidney beans and water and cook according to the Bean Cooking Chart (see page 11).

Heat the olive oil in a large cast-iron skillet over high heat. Add the garlic, shallot, and oregano and sauté for a minute or two. Stir in the rice until it is coated with the olive oil. Add the corn, cayenne pepper, and 1 teaspoon of salt. Stir in the stock, about $1/2$ cup at a time. Reduce the heat to medium and stir often. When the stock is absorbed, add another $1/2$ cup and stir. Continue to cook and stir, adding stock $1/2$ cup at a time, until the rice is soft and creamy. The risotto takes about 30 minutes to cook.

While the rice is cooking (and you are busy stirring), mix the tomato paste in with the cooked kidney beans. Add a small amount of water, if necessary. If the beans have some cooking liquid left after draining, you won't have to add water. When the rice is done, add the beans to the pan and mix. Add the nutritional yeast and mix. Add salt and pepper and adjust the seasonings.

Serve in individual bowls and garnish with the basil, black olives, and onion.

Curried Lentil Vegetable Stew

SERVES 4 TO 6

The spices used in this dish blend well so that no single flavor is overpowering. I don't care for a strong curry taste, so this dish is fairly mild. If you prefer it stronger tasting, increase the curry and cumin. This stew is great served over couscous.

2 to 3 tablespoons peanut oil

1 yellow onion, chopped

4 cloves garlic, minced

1 carrot, chopped

1/2 cauliflower, trimmed and cut into florets

2 red potatoes, chopped

1 cup fresh or frozen green peas

2 cups green lentils, rinsed

1 tablespoon freshly squeezed ginger juice (see page 5)

1 tablespoon curry powder

1 tablespoon garam masala

1 teaspoon turmeric

1 teaspoon ground cumin

1 teaspoon ground cinnamon

Pinch of cayenne pepper

3 tablespoons tamari

5 cups water

Sea salt

Heat the peanut oil in a large soup pot over high heat. Add the onion and garlic and quick sauté. Add the carrot and cauliflower and sauté for a few minutes, until the carrot brightens. Add the potatoes, peas, lentils, ginger juice, curry powder, garam masala, turmeric, cumin, cinnamon, and cayenne pepper and mix. Add the tamari and water.

Cover, bring to a boil, and simmer for approximately 45 minutes, until the lentils are cooked and the dish has a stewlike consistency.

Add salt and adjust seasonings. Serve hot.

Menu

This is a very hearty, warming meal that I usually serve in the winter. Because the stew is both flavorful and filling, I keep the other dishes of the meal very simple. I chose baked squash for a bit of sweetness and because it takes a while to cook, so it can bake while the stew is cooking. Bake the squash, halved and seeded, with a pinch of sea salt and a few drops of extra virgin olive oil at 450° for 1 hour. Poke it with a fork to make sure it is soft before serving.

Garbanzo Bean Stew with Eggplant and Tomato / 14

White Basmati Rice / 24

Baked Butternut Squash

**Green Salad with
Lemon Vinaigrette Dressing / 97**

Class 2: Whole Grains

**Part I: Rosie's
Cooking Classes**

Whole
Grains

AN INTRODUCTION TO WHOLE GRAINS

Whole grains comprise about 60 percent of my diet and are the basis for most vegetarian diets. They are tasty and nutritious, supplying vitamins, minerals, protein, and fiber. In contrast, refined grains such as white rice, couscous, or pearled barley are stripped of their bran and germ, causing a dramatic loss of nutrients. This is not to say never eat refined grains, as their taste is quite good; just don't eat them on a regular basis.

When thinking of whole grains most people think of brown rice, but the list of possible grains is lengthy. We have available to us many types of rice, including short, medium, and long-grain brown rice, arborio rice, sushi rice, sweet rice, and white and brown basmati rice. There are also amaranth, barley, buckwheat, bulgur, corn grits, kamut, millet, oats, quinoa, and spelt—and more. It's worth a trip to your local natural foods store just to see what these different grains look like. And then, of course, you can start experimenting with them. They all have distinctively different tastes and textures.

When cooking whole grains, you should first rinse them thoroughly to remove dirt, especially if you are buying from bulk bins. Some grains, like quinoa, need to be rinsed to remove their bitter natural coating. Choose a heavy pot (not aluminum) with a tight-fitting lid. Pour the grains into the pot, add cold water to cover, and swish the grains in a circular motion with your hand. Drain the water by pouring the grains into a colander. Return the grains to the pot, add the proper amount of water for cooking, add a pinch of sea salt, which enhances the flavor and improves the digestibility of the grains, and cover. Bring the water to a boil, then lower the heat to a simmer and continue to cook, covered, for the time specified in the Grain Cooking Chart (see page 24). There is no need to uncover the pot or mix the grains while they are cooking. When all of the water is absorbed, remove the grains from the pot and spoon them into a wooden or ceramic bowl to aerate before serving. The Grain Cooking Chart gives specific cooking times, but keep in mind that these times

may differ depending on the type of stove you use, the quantity of grains you cook, the simmering temperature, or heat escape due to lifting the lid while cooking. So use the chart as a guide when checking the grains for doneness. Use leftover grains in soups, stews, or burritos! They should last at least three days after cooking, if stored in the refrigerator.

GRAIN COOKING CHART

GRAIN (1 cup dry)	WATER (lightly salted) (cups)	COOKING TIME (minutes)	YIELD (cups)
Amaranth	2	25-30	2-2$^1/_2$
Barley, whole and hulled	3	90	3$^1/_2$-4
Barley, pearled	3	45	3$^1/_2$-4
Buckwheat groats	2	15	2-2$^1/_2$
Corn grits	3	20	3$^1/_2$-4
Kamut	3	120	2$^3/_4$
Millet	2$^1/_2$	25	3$^1/_2$-4
Oats, whole	3	60	3
Oats, rolled (oatmeal)	2	15	1$^1/_2$-2
Quinoa	2	20	3-3$^1/_2$
RICE			
Arborio*	2$^1/_2$	30	2-2$^1/_2$
Basmati, brown	2	45	3$^1/_2$
Basmati, white	1$^3/_4$	15	3$^1/_2$
Brown, short-, medium-, long-grain	2	45	2$^1/_2$-3
Sushi	2	45	2
Sweet	1$^1/_2$	45	2
Spelt	3	90-120	2$^1/_2$
WHEAT			
Whole berries	3	90-120	2$^1/_2$
Bulgur	2	15	2$^1/_2$
Couscous	2	1	2$^1/_2$-3

*Arborio rice must be stirred continually during cooking.

Lastly, a quick word about chewing. Grains need to be chewed more thoroughly than other foods for proper digestion. Many people switching to diets based on whole grains complain of gas and bloating because they don't chew their food well. It is important to relax at mealtime, slow down, sit down, and pay attention (and give thanks) for your food. It makes a tremendous difference.

" The average age (longevity) of a meat eater is 63.
I am on the verge of 85 and still work as hard as ever. I
have lived quite long enough and I am trying to die,
but I simply cannot do it. A single beef-steak would finish
me, but I cannot bring myself to swallow it. I am
oppressed with a dread of living forever. This is the only
disadvantage to vegetarianism. "
—George Bernard Shaw

Sesame Stir-Fry over Brown Rice

This is a simple recipe to begin your exploration of cooking with brown rice. It uses lots of fresh vegetables to produce a dish that is both colorful and tasty. This is a great dish for beginners to make to impress their guests!

1 cup short-grain brown rice

2 cups water

1 to 2 tablespoons toasted sesame oil

4 cloves garlic, chopped

1 yellow onion, halved and sliced

2 small yellow squash, trimmed and sliced

1 carrot, cut in matchsticks

2 to 3 tablespoons tamari

2 cups broccoli florets

1/2 small red cabbage, halved and thinly sliced

2 tablespoons freshly squeezed ginger juice (see page 5)

Unhulled sesame seeds for garnish

Combine the rice and water and cook according to the Grain Cooking Chart (see page 24).

Heat the oil in a cast-iron skillet over high heat. Add the garlic and onion and quick sauté for a few minutes. Add the squash, carrot, and tamari and sauté a few minutes more, or until the carrot brightens in color. Add the broccoli and continue to sauté for 5 minutes, or until the broccoli begins to turn a bright green color. Add the red cabbage. Sauté for 2 minutes, until the cabbage is bright in color. Stir in the ginger juice and sprinkle with sesame seeds.

Serve immediately over the rice.

Vegetable Medley over Basmati Rice

SERVES 4 TO 6

Although we don't use white basmati rice on a daily basis, it is a delicious tasting rice with a sort of nutty flavor. It goes especially well with garbanzo bean and lentil dishes.

1½ cups white basmati rice

3 cups water

1 pound brussels sprouts, trimmed and halved

2 to 3 tablespoons extra virgin olive oil

6 cloves garlic, halved

4 shiitake mushrooms, stemmed and sliced

½ butternut squash, seeded and cubed

1 carrot, cut in matchsticks

1 cup cooked garbanzo beans, rinsed and drained (see page 11)

1 cup packed chopped kale

1 cup soy milk

¼ cup tamari

¼ cup nutritional yeast

Toasted pumpkin seeds for garnish

Combine the rice and water and cook according to the Grain Cooking Chart (see page 24).

In a vegetable steamer, steam the brussels sprouts for 5 minutes, until bright green but still crisp. Set aside and let cool.

Heat the oil in a large cast-iron skillet over high heat. Add the garlic, mushrooms, butternut squash, and carrot and sauté for 5 minutes, until tender. Add the garbanzo beans and kale and sauté for a few minutes more, until the kale is bright green. Add the brussels sprouts and lower the heat.

In a bowl, mix together the soy milk, tamari, and nutritional yeast. Pour over the vegetable medley and cover. Remove from the heat and let stand for 1 to 2 minutes.

Garnish with pumpkin seeds and serve over the rice.

Winter Stew

This dish is named appropriately because I use mostly root vegetables that are readily available throughout the winter. It is a dish to warm you up, not something you would want to eat in the hot weather. The vegetables are sweet, giving the stew a mildly sweet but savory taste.

1 to 2 tablespoons light sesame oil

1 large white onion, diced

1 carrot, chopped

4 shiitake mushrooms, stemmed and sliced

1 parsnip, chopped

1/2 rutabaga, peeled and cubed

1 sweet potato, cubed

1 cup pearled barley, rinsed

2 bay leaves

1 teaspoon ground cumin

3 1/2 cups water

2 tablespoons chickpea or light barley miso (see page 38)

1 cup cooked navy beans, rinsed and drained (see page 11)

2 tablespoons freshly squeezed ginger juice (see page 5)

Fresh watercress for garnish

28

Part I: Rosie's Cooking Classes

Heat the oil in a large soup pot over high heat. Add the onion, carrot, and mushrooms and sauté for 1 minute. Add the parsnip, rutabaga, sweet potato, barley, bay leaves, cumin, and water. Cover, bring to a boil, and simmer for approximately 1 hour.

Remove 2 cups of the cooked vegetables and broth and blend in a food processor or blender with the miso until smooth. Return the mixture to the pot, add the beans and ginger juice, and let simmer for a few more minutes. Remove the bay leaves.

Serve in individual bowls and garnish with the watercress.

Quinoa with Corn and Onion

SERVES 4

The combination of quinoa and corn almost seems meant to be. This makes an excellent side dish in place of rice or pasta. Try adding some steamed, sliced asparagus or other vegetables of your choice, for more variety.

   1 cup quinoa, rinsed

   2 cups water

   1 cup fresh or frozen corn kernels

   1 to 2 tablespoons canola oil

   4 cloves garlic, minced

   1/2 red onion, chopped

   1 teaspoon dried basil

   Sea salt and freshly ground black pepper

   1 scallion, sliced thinly on the diagonal, for garnish

Combine the quinoa, water, and corn in a pot. Cover, bring to a boil, then lower the heat and simmer for 20 minutes.

Meanwhile, heat the oil in a cast-iron skillet over high heat. Add the garlic, onion, and basil and sauté for 5 to 8 minutes, until the onion turns translucent. Lower the heat and add the quinoa, corn, salt, and pepper. Mix well, remove from the heat, cover, and let stand for a few minutes before serving.

Serve with the scallion garnish.

66 *The most evolutionary thing we can commit to at this time is to become vegetarian.* 99

—*Albert Einstein (on a sign hanging at Max & Rosie's)*

RHONDA

There are places in the world where profundity and beauty merge into an experience you are not soon to forget. One such place is Café Max & Rosie's—a world of creativity and inspiration for both the soul and the taste buds. With food beyond delicious and an intimate environment that welcomes and warms you, each visit with Max and Rosie is one that brings a smile to the face and a lift to the heart. As part of that special place, I remember that every person was welcome, every smile counted, and every dish was an artistic creation. Not only were guests in great company with the magnificent paintings on the walls, but their

plates were palettes of color and texture. Max took great care in the preparation and placement of each crisp cucumber, each cascade of carrots, or rainbow of fresh fruit. Like his paintings, each was unique and an absolute delight. With Rosie's amazing culinary creations and Max's aesthetic brilliance, no place could seem more like home.

Rhonda was a student at the University of North Carolina at Asheville when she came into Max & Rosie's in search of a job. What a pleasure it was to meet someone so young, intelligent, and hardworking. She was rather quiet, a vegetarian, and a great believer in nonviolence. We talked many an hour about setting the world right. Although she was settled in domestic bliss for a while and was working on her Ph.D. in natural health, the last we heard from Rhonda, she was on her way to becoming a vet! We expect great things from her.

Rice and Mushroom Quesadilla

SERVES 4

We serve this dish at Max & Rosie's with chips and Jericho Salsa (see page 130). When avocados are in season, definitely include them. A big lunch hit.

- 2 cups brown rice
- 4 cups water
- 3 to 4 tablespoons canola oil
- 1/2 pound button mushrooms, trimmed and sliced
- 1 large yellow onion, chopped
- 2 teaspoons granulated garlic
- 4 (8-inch) flour or corn tortillas
- 1/2 pound pepper Jack–style soy cheese, thinly sliced
- 1 cup crumbled feta cheese (optional but very tasty)
- 2 ripe avocados, sliced, for garnish

Combine the rice and water and cook according to the Grain Cooking Chart (see page 24). When the rice is cooked, transfer it to a large bowl and let cool.

Heat 1 to 2 tablespoons of the oil in a cast-iron skillet over high heat. Add the mushrooms and onion, and sprinkle with the granulated garlic. Sauté for 5 to 8 minutes, until the onion is translucent. Set aside to cool.

Lay the tortillas flat on a work surface. Divide the rice into 4 equal portions and place a portion down the middle of each tortilla. Divide the mushrooms and onions into 4 portions and spoon a portion on top of each portion of rice. Sprinkle each tortilla with a quarter of the soy cheese and feta cheese. Fold the tortillas and turn them over.

Heat 2 tablespoons of oil in a large cast-iron skillet over high heat. Place the tortillas in the skillet, cover, reduce the heat to medium, and cook for 5 minutes, until the tortillas are browned.

Serve on individual plates garnished with the avocado.

Fried Rice with Seitan and Shiitake Mushrooms

SERVES 4 TO 6

This is an excellent dish in which to use your own favorite vegetables. The combination of seitan, shiitake mushrooms, and green peas is one of my favorites.

1 1/2 cups short-grain brown rice

3 cups water

2 to 3 tablespoons toasted sesame oil

8 cloves garlic, halved

1 leek, green and white parts, trimmed, cut lengthwise, and thinly sliced

4 shiitake mushrooms, stemmed and thinly sliced

6 brussels sprouts, trimmed and halved

1 carrot, chopped

1 cup frozen green peas

4 tablespoons tamari

1/2 pound teriyaki seitan, thinly sliced, retain the broth (see page 5)

2 cups chopped purple kale

Unhulled sesame seeds for garnish

Arugula leaves for garnish

Combine the rice and water and cook according to the Grain Cooking Chart (see page 24).

Heat the oil in a large cast-iron skillet over high heat. Add the garlic, leek, mushrooms, brussels sprouts, and carrot and sauté for 10 minutes. When the carrots are tender but still crispy, add the green peas and 2 tablespoons of the tamari and sauté for a few more minutes, until the peas are bright green. Add the seitan in its broth and stir. Add the kale, lower the heat, and cover for 2 minutes. When the kale is bright purple, remove the cover.

Transfer the cooked rice from the pot to a bowl and stir to let it aerate. Then add it to the skillet with the remaining 2 tablespoons tamari and mix with the vegetables.

Garnish with sesame seeds and arugula leaves. Serve immediately.

Millet Mashed Potatoes

SERVES 4 TO 6

This side dish is a jazzed-up version of mashed potatoes, made a lot more nutritious with the added millet and cauliflower. I highly recommend serving it with Mushroom Gravy (see page 104).

1 cup millet

2 to 3 tablespoons toasted sesame oil

1 small onion, chopped

2 cloves garlic, minced

2 russet potatoes, peeled and diced

1 small cauliflower, diced

3 1/4 cups water

2 teaspoons sweet paprika

1 teaspoon ground cumin

Pinch of cayenne pepper

3 tablespoons tahini

2 tablespoons tamari

Sea salt and freshly ground black pepper

Rinse the millet in a colander.

Heat the oil in a large pot over high heat. Add the onion and garlic and quick sauté for 2 to 3 minutes. Add the millet and stir. Add the potatoes and cauliflower. Sauté for another minute and add 3 cups of the water, the paprika, cumin, and cayenne pepper. Cover, bring to a boil, then lower the heat and simmer for 20 to 30 minutes, until all the water is absorbed.

While the millet is cooking, mix the tahini, the remaining 1/4 cup water, and tamari in a bowl and set aside.

When the millet mixture is cooked, mash it with a potato masher. Add the tahini mixture and mix well. Add salt and pepper. Adjust the seasonings and serve.

Menu

Although this menu is based on brown rice, it has many different and interesting flavors. You don't have to add much to a dish like this, so I simply begin with a light, creamy soup and serve the fried rice with a steamed vegetable and salad.

Potato Leek Soup / 76

Fried Rice with Seitan and Shiitake Mushrooms / 33

Steamed Broccoli

Tossed Salad
with Lemon Tahini Dressing / 96

Class 3: Soy (Tofu and Tempeh)

Soy

AN INTRODUCTION TO SOY

Soy foods are becoming more and more popular today. People that used to cringe at the thought of tofu are now enjoying it at mealtime. Soy foods have come a long way in both availability and taste, as you will see when cooking the recipes in this class.

Soy has been shown to slow the growth of certain cancers, contain immune boosters and antioxidants, help prevent heart disease, and lower blood cholesterol. Soy is high in protein and rich in other essential nutrients, including calcium, iron, zinc, and B vitamins.

Tofu, also known as soybean curd, is a soft, cheeselike food. It is remarkably nutritious, easy to digest, and relatively inexpensive. Tofu comes in various forms, categorized according to water content: extra firm, firm, soft, and silken. The firmer the tofu, the less water it contains and the better it holds its shape in cooking. The firmer forms of tofu work best in stir-fries and casseroles, while the softer forms are best in loaves, dips, and dressings. Silken tofu is best in puréed or blended dishes. Fresh tofu has little or no smell, and it basically has no taste. It takes on the flavors of the foods, herbs, and spices it is cooked with. So cooking with tofu can be a creative work of art for you!

Tempeh is made of whole cooked soybeans injected with a culture and fermented. This fermentation process makes the soy protein more digestible. Tempeh comes in a variety of flavors, including soy, three-grain, five-grain, quinoa, amaranth, and sea vegetable, and there is a dramatic variation in taste and texture among the different types. I usually use soy tempeh, as it has a bit more protein as well as a nice flavor. Tempeh comes frozen or refrigerated, usually in an 8-ounce patty. It naturally has a slightly bitter taste, and I usually season it with tamari and spices before cooking. My personal preference for cooking tempeh is to fry it until crispy. It can also be baked or broiled, but make sure it is thoroughly cooked or the flavor will definitely suffer.

Tamari, soy sauce, and shoyu are similar in taste and used interchangeably in recipes. They are fermented from soybeans, wheat, and

Class 3: Soy

fermenting agents for about 18 months. However, there are also chemically processed soy sauces that should be avoided. If you have a wheat allergy, look for wheat-free versions. Tamari is very salty and although I use it a lot, especially in marinades, it should be used in small quantities or mixed with other liquids, as the flavor can be overpowering.

Miso is a fermented soybean paste high in B vitamins and protein. Miso that is purchased refrigerated contains live enzymes that aid in digestion and should never be boiled. Miso comes in different varieties, such as barley miso, chickpea miso, brown rice miso, white rice miso, and others. They each have a distinctively different flavor and should be used accordingly. Most people have had traditional miso soup, served in Japanese restaurants, but miso is also good for flavoring stews, sauces, marinades, and dressings. It has a strong flavor, so go easy with it.

There are many soy products on the market today that weren't available when I became a vegetarian. As a matter of fact, I was making my own tofu back in the seventies and had never heard of tempeh. But today we have so many things available to us, such as soy milk, soy cheese, tofu "hot dogs," tofu "baloney," soy yogurt, soy mayonnaise, and the list goes on and on. A far cry from the days of rice and beans!

So enjoy these recipes. And try some of the soy products on the market. Your body will thank you.

Part I: Rosie's Cooking Classes

66 *Owning a vegetarian café, I am surrounded, for the most part, by people who are conscious of their eating habits, and so I forget how the majority of this country still eats. I was talking with a teenage boy at our local supermarket about being vegetarian and he said, "Oh, I could never do that. I like meat too much." He was about 40 pounds overweight and had a noticeable shortness of breath.* 99
—*Rosie*

Tofu Burgers

SERVES 4

These burgers have a nice, nutty flavor with a crunchy consistency. This recipe calls for frying, but you can also bake them on a lightly oiled cookie sheet at 350° for approximately 15 minutes on each side. Personally, I like the burgers crispy, which means a little extra cooking time. If they seem a bit oily, drain them on paper towels before serving. They are great served on a bun with lots of veggies and your favorite condiments.

- 1 pound firm tofu, drained and mashed
- 1/4 cup tamari
- 2 tablespoons water
- 2 tablespoons tahini
- 1/4 cup rolled oats
- 1/4 cup unbleached all-purpose flour
- 1/2 cup whole-wheat flour
- 1/4 onion, chopped
- 1 stalk celery, chopped
- 2 tablespoons sunflower seeds
- 1 teaspoon granulated garlic
- 1/2 teaspoon dried basil
- 1 teaspoon dried oregano
- 1/4 teaspoon freshly ground black pepper
- 1/2 cup unhulled sesame seeds
- Canola oil for frying

Combine the tofu, tamari, water, and tahini in a large mixing bowl. Add the oats, all-purpose and whole-wheat flours, onion, celery, sunflower seeds, garlic, basil, oregano, and pepper. Mix well. Form into 4 patties (not too thick) and lightly dip them in the sesame seeds.

Heat 1/2 inch of canola oil in a large cast-iron skillet over medium-high heat. When the oil is hot, brown the patties for 5 minutes on each side. You may want to press down on them with a metal spatula to make sure they cook through. Watch out for the sesame seeds; they tend to pop. Serve hot on a bun.

Scrambled Tofu

SERVES 4 TO 6

This dish is a great alternative to scrambled eggs for breakfast. It is very tasty, high in protein, and free of cholesterol. It's great for breakfast with toast or as a quick meal with some leftover grains and steamed greens or salad.

2 to 3 tablespoons light sesame oil

1 yellow onion, chopped

2 cloves garlic, finely chopped

2 scallions, whites and greens separated and thinly sliced

6 button mushrooms, thinly sliced

2 pounds firm tofu, drained and mashed

1/4 cup tamari

1/2 teaspoon dried oregano

1/2 teaspoon turmeric

Sea salt and freshly ground black pepper

Heat the oil in a large cast-iron skillet over high heat. Add the onion, garlic, and scallion whites and sauté for 8 to 10 minutes, until the onion is translucent. Add the mushrooms, tofu, tamari, oregano, and turmeric and continue to sauté over medium heat, stirring frequently, for 5 minutes, or until the tofu is yellow and resembles scrambled eggs. Stir in the scallion greens and salt and pepper. Serve at once.

66 *Giving up meat will end the vile treatment of animals (factory farming). Could this inhumane treatment of animals be anything but physically, mentally, and spiritually destructive to humankind?* 99
—*Max*

Tofu Cutlets

SERVES 4

If you are looking for a dinner "meat substitute" that seems similar to a piece of fish or chicken, here it is. It's great with Millet Mashed Potatoes (see page 34). You can also try it with baked potatoes and salad, or rice and steamed vegetables. It makes a good sandwich as well. This is one of those recipes for people who think they hate tofu!

1 pound firm tofu

1/2 cup tamari

1 tablespoon tahini

2 tablespoons freshly squeezed ginger juice (see page 5)

1 1/2 cups whole-wheat flour

1/2 cup nutritional yeast

2 teaspoons granulated garlic

2 to 3 tablespoons canola oil

Chopped scallion greens for garnish

Slice the tofu into 4 equal slices and then cut each slice diagonally in half, so that you have 8 triangular pieces. In a shallow dish, mix together the tamari, tahini, and ginger juice. Add the tofu and marinate it in this mixture for 15 to 30 minutes.

Mix the flour, nutritional yeast, and garlic on a flat plate and set aside.

Heat the oil in a large cast-iron skillet over medium-high heat. Dip the marinated tofu in the flour mixture to coat both sides. Fry for 3 to 5 minutes on each side, turning once, until browned and crispy. If the tofu begins to stick, add a little more oil.

Serve immediately with the scallion garnish.

MARTI

I've always appreciated the fact that Max and Rosie hired me even though I had absolutely no experience in restaurant work. (Hell, I can't even boil water!) But, Rosie is a genius with natural foods and kitchen rookies, and even though I never learned the secret recipe for her sumptuous veggie burger, I did learn how to crank out hundreds of them. I also had the time of my life in that little café.

I actually went to the café to recover from burnout—the occasional curse of a busy therapist, but I realized as I spit-polished that black-and-white checkered kitchen floor every night that I had a little obsessive-compulsive disorder of my own and could turn any job into a high-stress proposition.

That's where Max came in. He was my therapist. He taught me how to laugh at myself, how to have a full-blown argument and completely make up all during a busy lunch hour, how a good marriage and a healthy family operate, and that if people are talking about you behind your back, you've probably done something right.

I am a therapist again now, and I adore my work, but I still think about my days at the café. There is something deeply rewarding about feeding hungry people, whether that hunger lives in the soul or in the belly. And there is something very special about connecting with others, whether it's over the pain of living or the joy of a good veggie sandwich.

Marti came into our café early on. She was a therapist in search of a sabbatical. She became our ace sandwich maker. Her pace reminded us a bit of the Road Runner. She would never just walk into the café to begin work. She would literally dash in and do long sweeps with her dishcloth along the sandwich unit. The floor was in competition with the sandwich unit for how much food could accumulate there. She was a neurotic delight.

Her love affairs were so extreme that we became exhausted by their gyrations. But, as Marti said, "With 100 percent of the population to choose from, I will find my soul mate." Many years later, after extricating herself from a Mafia-run hospital, she met her true love and, God willing, she will live happily ever after. She is the only person we've ever known who would still be at the café cleaning at midnight—after the kitchen closed at 6 P.M. We love you Marti.

Tofu and Broccoli in Garlic Sauce

SERVES 4 TO 6

Broccoli in garlic sauce is one of my favorite dishes to eat at Chinese restaurants. It is hard to match the sweetness without using sugar, but the garlic and chili peppers give it a nice zip. I don't usually serve the peppers after the dish is cooked; if you do, provide a warning. They're quite hot.

1^1/2 cups short-grain brown rice

3 cups water

^{1}/4 cup tamari

2 tablespoons balsamic vinegar

1 pound firm tofu, drained and cubed

3 to 5 tablespoons toasted sesame oil

1 onion, halved and sliced

12 cloves garlic, chopped

4 shiitake mushrooms, stemmed and thinly sliced

1 carrot, cut in matchsticks

1 cup vegetable stock (see page 67) or water

1 tablespoon Dijon mustard

3 tablespoons honey

2 tablespoons freshly squeezed ginger juice (see page 5)

2 dried chiles

2 cups broccoli florets

1 tablespoon kuzu or arrowroot

Unhulled sesame seeds for garnish

Combine the rice and water and cook according to the Grain Cooking Chart (see page 24).

Combine the tamari and vinegar in a shallow dish. Add the tofu and marinate it for 30 minutes. Drain and reserve the liquid.

Heat 2 to 3 tablespoons of the oil in a large cast-iron skillet over medium-high heat. Add the tofu and brown it on all sides for 8 to 10 minutes.

Remove the tofu and set it aside. Add the remaining 1 to 2 tablespoons of oil and the onion, garlic, mushrooms, and carrot to the pan. Sauté for 5 minutes, or until the carrots brighten but are still crispy.

In a small bowl, mix the stock, mustard, honey, and ginger juice and add it to the skillet. Stir. Add the chiles. Add the tofu and reserved tamari and vinegar. Then add the broccoli. Simmer, covered, for 3 to 5 minutes, until the broccoli is bright green in color.

Dissolve the kuzu in a small amount of cold water and add it to the skillet while stirring. Simmer over medium heat for 1 to 2 minutes.

Serve hot over the rice. Garnish with sesame seeds.

Note: As a general rule of thumb, use 1 tablespoon kuzu or arrowroot per cup of liquid for sauces or gravies. Always dissolve it in cold liquid before using.

Tofu Chili

The tofu gives this vegetarian chili a meatlike consistency. You can also use tempeh in place of the tofu. Make sure to adjust the spices to your taste. This recipe is medium hot. Serve with crackers or crusty bread.

1/4 cup tamari

2 tablespoons plus 1/2 to 1 cup water

2 tablespoons tahini

2 teaspoons granulated garlic

2 pounds firm tofu, drained and mashed

1/2 cup canola oil

1 green bell pepper, chopped

1 large yellow onion, chopped

4 cloves garlic, minced

4 cups cooked kidney beans, rinsed and drained (see page 11)

1 (15-ounce) can tomato paste

2 red chiles, seeded and chopped

2 tablespoons chili powder

Sea salt and freshly ground black pepper

In a bowl, mix together the tamari, 2 tablespoons water, tahini, and garlic. Add the tofu and mix until the tofu is evenly coated.

Heat the oil in a large cast-iron skillet over medium-high heat. Add the tofu and brown it on all sides, turning with a wooden or metal spatula. Transfer the tofu to a large soup pot. Add the green pepper, onion, and garlic to the skillet and sauté for approximately 5 minutes. Add to the pot.

Add the beans and tomato paste to the soup pot. Add 1/2 to 1 cup water to thin the chili to a desired consistency. Add the chiles and chili powder and simmer, covered, for at least 30 minutes. Add salt and pepper and adjust the seasonings.

Serve hot.

Braised Tempeh and Cabbage

SERVES 4 TO 6

This recipe, with some adjustments, was one of the first macrobiotic dishes I learned to cook, so I guess I've been making this for about 15 years. And I'm still enjoying it!

2 (8-ounce) pieces tempeh, cubed

1/4 cup tamari

2 tablespoons plus 1/2 cup water

5 to 8 tablespoons toasted sesame oil

6 cloves garlic, finely chopped

1/2 yellow onion, thinly sliced

1 carrot, cut in matchsticks

1/2 savoy or napa cabbage, trimmed and thinly sliced

2 tablespoons Dijon mustard

3 tablespoons freshly squeezed ginger juice (see page 5)

Unhulled sesame seeds for garnish

Scallion greens, thinly sliced on the diagonal, for garnish

In a small bowl, combine the tempeh, tamari, and 2 tablespoons water. Let this sit for just a few minutes or the flavor will become too salty. Drain and reserve the liquid.

Heat 4 to 6 tablespoons of the oil in a large cast-iron skillet over high heat. Add the tempeh and fry until it is golden on all sides. Remove the tempeh from the pan and set it aside. Add the remaining 1 to 2 tablespoons of oil, the garlic, onion, and carrot to the pan and sauté for 5 minutes, until the carrot brightens. Add the cabbage and stir.

In a bowl, mix together the mustard, ginger juice, 1/2 cup water, and reserved tamari mixture. Add to the skillet. Cover and simmer for approximately 5 minutes. Remove the cover, add the tempeh, and sprinkle with sesame seeds and sliced scallion.

Serve immediately over rice or Japanese noodles.

Lemon-Ginger Tempeh
with Onions and Mushrooms

SERVES 4 TO 6

This tempeh dish has a nice bite to it. You may want to adjust the amounts of lemon and ginger if it is too strongly flavored for you. This makes a great main dish with rice or potatoes and steamed broccoli and carrots.

2 (8-ounce) pieces tempeh

$1/2$ cup freshly squeezed lemon juice

$1/4$ cup freshly squeezed ginger juice (see page 5)

2 tablespoons tamari

2 to 3 tablespoons toasted sesame oil

1 to 2 tablespoons extra virgin olive oil

1 large onion, chopped

$1/2$ pound button mushrooms, trimmed and sliced

Fresh parsley for garnish

Lemon wedges for garnish

Cut each tempeh patty in half. Cut each half patty in half again, diagonally, so that there are 8 trianglular pieces. In a bowl, mix together the lemon and ginger juices and the tamari.

Heat the sesame oil in a large cast-iron skillet over high heat. Add the tempeh and begin to brown. Slowly cover the tempeh with the lemon juice mixture. Be careful, as this will splatter. Brown the tempeh for 5 minutes on each side.

In a separate skillet, heat the olive oil over medium-high heat. Add the onion and mushrooms and sauté for 5 minutes, until the onion is translucent.

Transfer the tempeh to a serving platter and spoon the onion and mushrooms over the tempeh. Garnish the platter with parsley sprigs and lemon wedges and serve.

Menu

This menu makes a delicious dinner, and as it is a grand meal, I suggest a small dinner party, perhaps with a nice bottle of Australian Merlot. Be sure to allow yourself enough time to prepare this meal; it is definitely not something you would whip up after work. You may even want to prepare the soup the day before to save time. To prepare the green beans and rutabaga, cut the rutabaga into 1-inch cubes and steam it 5 to 10 minutes. Add the green beans and steam 5 minutes more.

Split Pea and Garlic Soup / 75

Tofu Cutlets / 44

**Millet Mashed Potatoes / 34
with Mushroom Gravy / 104**

Steamed Green Beans and Rutabaga

**Green Salad with
Lemon Basil Dressing / 101**

Class 4: Pastas

Pastas

AN INTRODUCTION TO PASTAS

After many years of cooking macrobiotically and many objections from our children about eating so much brown rice ("Brown rice again?"), I began to branch out to pastas. Initially I served udon and soba noodles with a macrobiotic flair. But gradually the Italian side of pasta cooking really caught me. We started eating spaghetti, linguine, fettuccine, penne, angel-hair, lasagne, and lots of olive oil and garlic. For a while it seemed I could not get enough of it. But when I started hearing, "Pasta again?" I realized I may have gone a bit overboard. Remember, variety in cooking is extremely important. And even though I tend to want the same thing for quite a while before tiring of it, there is my family to consider.

Different types of pasta cook in different lengths of time. Aside from Japanese udon and soba noodles, I cook with DeBoles brand organic pastas, which combine semolina and Jerusalem artichoke flours and have a nicer flavor and texture than the traditional semolina pastas. The cooking times vary with each type of pasta, so follow the cooking instructions on the package. However, general pasta cooking instructions are as follows: Use 4 quarts of lightly salted water per pound of pasta. Bring the water to a boil in a covered stainless steel pot. Remove the lid and add the pasta to the water, a little at a time. Stir immediately so the pasta doesn't stick. Let the water return to a boil and cook until the pasta is al dente. Drain in a colander. Depending on the recipe, either rinse the pasta with water or toss with sauce or other ingredients. Although my recipes name a specific pasta to use, you can choose whatever you like. For example, the vegan pesto sauce (see page 53) goes great with penne as well as fettuccine.

My pasta dishes are usually complete meals in themselves because they contain vegetables and either tempeh, tofu, seitan, or beans. I present them with a word of warning. I love garlic and use a lot of it in my recipes. If it is too much for you, use less or cut it out completely. I realize garlic is not for everyone. A tossed salad and a nice crusty bread, or a baked garlic bread (you see?) rounds out a pasta meal nicely. Serving the pasta on a large platter with the vegetables on top and a nice garnish makes for a beautiful presentation.

Spaghetti with Tempeh Sauce

SERVES 4 TO 6

This is actually a mock "meat sauce" and it definitely has that consistency. Feel free to substitute your favorite bottled marinara sauce for the tomato sauce and paste, keeping all other ingredients the same. If you want more of a vegetable sauce, sauté zucchini, eggplant, or other vegetables and add them to the sauce.

3 to 5 tablespoons extra virgin olive oil

1 large yellow onion, chopped

6 cloves garlic, minced

2 ripe plum tomatoes, chopped

1/2 pound button mushrooms or one large portobello, trimmed and thinly sliced

2 tablespoons dried oregano

1/2 cup chopped fresh basil or 2 teaspoons dried basil

1 (8-ounce) piece soy tempeh, crumbled

2 tablespoons tamari

2 teaspoons granulated garlic

2 (15-ounce) cans tomato sauce

1 (6-ounce) can tomato paste

1 pound spaghetti

1/4 cup nutritional yeast

Sea salt and freshly ground black pepper

Heat 1 to 2 tablespoons of the oil in a cast-iron skillet over high heat. Add the onion, garlic, tomatoes, mushrooms, oregano, and basil and quick sauté for 2 to 3 minutes. Transfer to a saucepan.

In a shallow dish, mix the tempeh with the tamari and granulated garlic. Heat the remaining 2 to 3 tablespoons of oil in the skillet over high heat. Add the seasoned tempeh and fry, turning with a spatula, until brown. Transfer this to the saucepan. Add the tomato sauce and paste (or your favorite jar of marinara sauce) and stir. Cover, reduce the heat, and simmer for a minimum of 30 minutes.

While the sauce is simmering, cook the pasta according to package directions. Drain well.

Add the nutritional yeast, salt, and pepper to the sauce. Adjust the seasonings. If the sauce is too thick, you can add a little water. Serve hot over the pasta.

Fettuccine with Vegan Pesto Sauce

SERVES 4 TO 6

Pesto is a traditional Italian sauce, usually made with Parmesan cheese. I use nutritional yeast in place of the cheese. Use this sauce in moderation, as it has a delicious but strong flavor. I do suggest you play with the measurements, as you may want more of a garlic flavor, or more olive oil for a smoother consistency. I strongly suggest you use a food processor for this recipe, as a blender is much more labor intensive.

4 cloves garlic

1 1/2 cups packed fresh basil leaves

3/4 cup nutritional yeast

3/4 cup extra virgin olive oil

1/4 cup pignoli (pine nuts)

Sea salt and freshly ground black pepper

1 pound fettuccine

Mince the garlic in a food processor. Add the basil, nutritional yeast, oil, and pine nuts, and blend until you have a desired consistency. Season with salt and pepper.

Cook the fettuccine according to package directions. Drain well and toss with the pesto sauce. Serve immediately.

Spaghetti Squash in Olive Oil and Garlic

SERVES 4

This isn't quite a pasta dish, although I include it in the pasta cooking class at the café. Spaghetti squash is quite stringy, not unlike pasta, and is great for pasta lovers with or without wheat allergies! This makes a delicious, quick side dish.

1 spaghetti squash, seeded and halved

1 to 2 tablespoons extra virgin olive oil

6 cloves garlic, minced

2 tablespoons nutritional yeast

Sea salt and freshly ground black pepper

Fresh flat-leaf parsley sprigs for garnish

Steam the squash until soft, about 15 minutes. Let cool a bit and remove the filling from its shell.

Heat the oil in a cast-iron skillet over medium-high heat. Add the garlic and squash and sauté for 5 minutes, making sure the squash retains its yellow color. Add the nutritional yeast, salt, and pepper.

Serve garnished with a few sprigs of fresh parsley.

> *To be a vegetarian is to disagree—to disagree with the course of things today. Starvation, world hunger, cruelty, waste, wars—we must make a statement against these things. Vegetarianism is my statement. And I think it's a strong one.*
> —Isaac Bashevis Singer

Linguine with Fresh Garlic and Asparagus

Another hit at our house. It is a light pasta dish, like an aglio e olio, *but with a lot less oil. It is nice to serve in the warmer weather with a mixed salad. I use Bragg Liquid Aminos (see note) instead of tamari in this dish because the flavor is not as strong.*

1 pound linguine

1/4 cup Bragg Liquid Aminos

1 tablespoon balsamic vinegar

2 teaspoons granulated garlic

1 (8-ounce) piece soy tempeh, cubed

1 portobello mushroom, trimmed and sliced

5 tablespoons extra virgin olive oil

1 pound fresh asparagus, trimmed and halved crosswise

8 cloves garlic, minced

Sea salt

1 to 2 tablespoons water

2 cups fresh baby spinach

1/2 cup coarsely chopped fresh basil

Fresh basil leaves for garnish

Dressing for Pasta:

1/2 cup extra virgin olive oil

1 tablespoon umeboshi vinegar (optional)

2 tablespoons nutritional yeast

2 tablespoons water

Freshly ground black pepper

Cook the linguine according to package directions. Drain, rinse under cold water, and set aside in the pot with cold water to cover. This will keep it from sticking.

Café Max & Rosie's

56

Part I: Rosie's
Cooking Classes

Mix the Bragg liquid aminos, balsamic vinegar, and granulated garlic in a bowl. Add the tempeh and mushroom slices and toss.

Heat 4 tablespoons of the oil in a cast-iron skillet over high heat. Add the tempeh and mushroom slices and fry for about 10 minutes. Turn each tempeh cube as the sides brown and become crispy. (This can be a bit tedious but it is important. Undercooked tempeh is not a pretty sight, nor does it taste good.) Turn the mushrooms over once while the tempeh is cooking. Remove the tempeh and mushrooms from the skillet and set aside.

Heat 1 tablespoon of the oil in the skillet over medium-high heat. Add the asparagus and the minced garlic and stir. Add a sprinkle of salt and 1 to 2 tablespoons of water as necessary, especially if the garlic is sticking to the skillet. Stir frequently for about 5 minutes. Then turn off the heat and cover for a few minutes, making sure the asparagus stays bright green. When the asparagus is tender but still crisp (test with a fork), add the baby spinach, fresh basil, and a pinch more salt. Cover to let the spinach and basil wilt.

Meanwhile, mix the dressing for the pasta by combining the oil, vinegar, nutritional yeast, and water in a small bowl.

Drain the pasta and immediately toss with the dressing. If it's too dry, add a bit more oil and vinegar. Add salt, if necessary, and pepper.

Transfer the pasta to a large platter and arrange the asparagus, spinach, tempeh, and mushrooms on top. Garnish with fresh basil leaves. Serve immediately.

Note: Bragg Liquid Aminos can be found in most health food stores in 16 and 32-ounce bottles. If it is not available, you can substitute 3 tablespoons of tamari mixed with 1 tablespoon of water for the 1/4 cup of Bragg.

Pasta Primavera

SERVES 4 TO 6

I like to use angel-hair pasta for this dish because it is so light, it takes the background to the bright, fresh vegetables. I often make this with tempeh cubes instead of the beans.

2 to 3 tablespoons extra virgin olive oil

6 cloves garlic, minced

1 red bell pepper, seeded and thinly sliced

2 ripe plum tomatoes, chopped

$^1/2$ pound asparagus, trimmed and halved crosswise

1 yellow squash, cut in matchsticks

2 cups broccoli florets

1 tablespoon dried oregano

2 cups cooked white beans, rinsed and drained (see page 11) (optional)

1 cup coarsely chopped fresh basil leaves

Sea salt and freshly ground black pepper

1 pound angel-hair pasta

Fresh basil leaves for garnish

Dressing for Pasta

1 cup extra virgin olive oil

$^1/4$ cup balsamic vinegar

3 tablespoons umeboshi vinegar

4 tablespoons nutritional yeast

Heat the oil in a large cast-iron skillet over high heat. Add the garlic, red pepper, tomato, and asparagus and sauté for 3 to 5 minutes making sure the red pepper and asparagus remain crisp. Add the yellow squash, broccoli, and oregano and sauté for another 3 minutes, or until the broccoli is bright green. Add the white beans and stir. Add the chopped basil. Cover and turn off the heat. Let stand for a few minutes, then remove the cover. Be sure to keep the colors of the vegetables bright, so they do not overcook. Adjust the seasonings.

Meanwhile, cook the pasta according to the package directions. Angel-hair pasta takes only a few minutes.

Mix the dressing for the pasta by combining the oil, vinegars, and yeast. Mix well.

When the pasta is cooked, drain and immediately toss it with the dressing.

Transfer the pasta to a platter and top with the vegetables and beans. Garnish with fresh basil. Serve immediately.

" *Take fresh ingredients and let them breathe through the cooking process. Now that's real cooking.* "
—*Rosie*

Penne with Tofu and Vegetables

SERVES 4 TO 6

This dish is actually a variation of pasta primavera. If you vary your pastas and vegetables, you can come up with quite a variety of pasta dishes. The cornmeal in this recipe gives the tofu a very distinctive taste.

1 pound penne pasta

1 pound firm tofu, cubed

1 cup tamari

2 to 3 tablespoons extra virgin olive oil

8 cloves garlic, halved

1 small leek, white and green parts, cut lengthwise and sliced

1 carrot, cut in matchsticks

4 shiitake mushrooms, stemmed and thinly sliced

6 brussels sprouts, trimmed and halved

1/2 pound fresh green beans, trimmed and halved crosswise

Cornmeal for breading tofu

1/4 cup canola oil

2 tablespoons Bragg Liquid Aminos (or substitute 1 tablespoon tamari and 1 tablespoon water)

1/2 cup nutritional yeast

Sea salt and freshly ground black pepper

Unhulled sesame seeds for garnish

Cook the penne according to package directions. Drain, rinse under cold water, and set aside in the pot with cold water to cover. This will keep it from sticking.

Place the tofu in a bowl with the tamari. Mix and set aside.

Heat the olive oil in a large cast-iron skillet over high heat. Add the garlic, leek, carrot, and mushrooms and sauté for 2 to 3 minutes, until the carrot brightens. Add the brussels sprouts and green beans and sauté for 5 to 8 minutes, until the vegetables are crisp, tender, and bright in color. Remove from heat.

Dredge the tofu in enough cornmeal to cover all the pieces.

Heat the canola oil in a separate skillet and fry the tofu on all sides for about 10 minutes, until crispy. Drain on paper towels.

Drain the pasta well, and toss gently with the Bragg. Reheat the vegetable skillet, add the pasta, and mix. Add the nutritional yeast and toss gently. Add salt and pepper. When the pasta is warm, place the tofu cubes on top and garnish with a sprinkle of sesame seeds. Serve immediately.

Udon Stir-Fry in a Vegan Cream Sauce

SERVES 4 TO 6

This dish is a sort of vegan "Udon Alfredo" with vegetables. Udon is a traditional Japanese noodle. It is a thick, cream-colored wheat noodle. Be careful not to overcook it, because it will turn mushy. Make sure you serve this dish immediately so the sauce doesn't dry out.

1 pound udon noodles

3 to 4 tablespoons toasted sesame oil or hot pepper sesame oil or
   a combination of the two

4 shiitake mushrooms, stemmed and thinly sliced

1 sweet potato, peeled and cubed

4 brussels sprouts, stemmed and halved

1/2 pound teriyaki seitan, thinly sliced, retain the broth (see page 5)

2 cups broccoli florets

1 cup chopped kale

Slivered almonds for garnish

Sauce

1 1/2 tablespoons light sesame oil

1 shallot, finely chopped

4 cloves garlic, minced

2 tablespoons tamari

2 teaspoons mirin (sweet Japanese rice wine)

1 tablespoon tahini

1 1/2 cups soy milk

3 tablespoons arrowroot or kuzu

1/2 cup cold water

Freshly ground black pepper

Cook the udon according to package directions. Drain, rinse under cold water, and set aside in the pot with cold water to cover. This will keep it from sticking.

Heat the oil in a large cast-iron skillet over medium-high heat. Add the mushrooms, sweet potato, and brussels sprouts and sauté for about 10 minutes, adding a small amount of water if the vegetables stick. Check the sweet potato with a fork. When it is crisp but tender, add the seitan with its broth and toss. Lower the heat, add the broccoli and kale, and cover. Steam for 2 minutes, or until the broccoli and kale turn bright green. Remove from heat.

Meanwhile, prepare the sauce. Heat the oil in a saucepan over medium heat. Add the shallot and garlic and stir. Combine the tamari, mirin, and tahini in a small bowl and add to the saucepan. Stir. Add the soy milk, lower the heat, and cover.

Dissolve the arrowroot in 1/2 cup cold water. When the sauce comes almost to a boil, add the arrowroot, and stir until thick, about 1 minute. Add black pepper to taste.

Rinse the cooked udon noodles under hot water and drain well. Toss with the vegetables and seitan. Arrange on a platter and top with the sauce. Garnish with slivered almonds. Serve immediately.

> **If you're not vegetarian, you're part of the problem.**
> **If you are vegetarian, you're part of the solution.**
> **Better personal health, better planetary health.**
> **—Max**

SOL

Coming into Max & Rosie's is like coming into a new dimension. The ambiance and the food complement each other. Being with people and doing my thing (kidding around) keeps me going; it's my medicine. Since I've been helping out at the café I've seen the business grow and take some new directions. (Could I have had anything to do with that?) I'm very proud of my daughter and son-in-law for creating this unique and successful café. Of course, for my daughter, it is in her blood. (What can I say? She's my daughter!) The future looks very bright for Café Max & Rosie's.

Sol had spent his whole life owning and working in different coffee shops. Then Sol and Eddi decided to move up from Florida to be closer to their children and grandchildren. They had retired, but within two weeks of being in Asheville, Sol was down at Max & Rosie's helping out.

Watching Sol behind the counter is rather like watching Rembrandt paint a portrait. He is a real master. To watch him work is to see love in action. He loves the people, he loves being here, and he loves the business. (And, by the way, the people genuinely love him!) If you come to Max & Rosie's, make sure to catch his "coin trick." Customers ask for it daily.

As Rosie's parents, Sol and Eddi give from their hearts to help us on our working journey. We are blessed to have them here.

Menu

Most meals that I make with pasta need only the addition of a green salad and sometimes garlic bread, because the pasta dishes already include vegetables and tofu or tempeh. In this menu, I serve minestrone soup first, as it has the vegetables and beans that the pasta dish is lacking. The asparagus mellows the pesto flavor a bit and the red pepper adds some color. Steam the asparagus right before serving the meal. I prefer it still crunchy with this meal.

Minestrone Soup / 68

Fettuccine with Vegan Pesto Sauce / 53

Steamed Asparagus

Sliced Red Bell Pepper

Tossed Salad
with Lemon Vinaigrette Dressing / 97

Class 5: Souper Soups

Café Max & Rosie's

66

Part I: Rosie's
Cooking Classes

Souper
Soups

AN INTRODUCTION TO SOUPS

Cooking soups is one of my favorite things to do. It's one of those things that is so simple, yet allows for such creativity. You can usually make soup with what you have on hand, including leftovers. Depending on what you put in it, soup very often can be a meal in itself.

It is best to start soup with stock, and there is nothing better for making stock than vegetable scraps. Just save the stalks of broccoli, asparagus, ends of summer squash, limp carrots, onion peels, etc., in the refrigerator until you have enough for a stock (at least half of your soup pot). Scraps can be saved for a week. Chop the scraps, put them in the pot, and cover with water. Cover the pot, add your favorite herbs and spices to make the stock more flavorful, bring to a boil, and then simmer for 60 to 90 minutes. Drain off the liquid using a colander, discard the vegetables, and begin your soup with this stock. Although this is optional in preparing soup, your soups will be much tastier starting with stock than beginning with water.

Most of the recipes that follow have you sauté vegetables and then add the rest of the ingredients to complete the soup. Please note that sautéing does add flavor to the soup, but it is not necessary, especially if you are concerned about the oil.

If you don't have the exact ingredients on hand for these recipes, or any other soups that you may prepare, substitute something else. If you don't like a particular vegetable or bean in a recipe, use something else. Hopefully, you will get to the point of looking in your refrigerator, using the vegetables you find, maybe adding leftover grains, beans, pastas, and so on, seasoning to taste, and creating your own mouthwatering soups. Just remember to be creative and enjoy.

Minestrone Soup

SERVES 4 TO 6

This is a hearty winter soup, and it is pretty much a meal in itself. It is traditionally made with kidney beans, but I like to use garbanzo beans as well. Serve it for lunch or dinner with a green salad and crusty bread.

2 to 3 tablespoons extra virgin olive oil

4 cloves garlic, minced

1/2 large yellow onion, chopped

1 carrot, cut lengthwise and sliced

1 cup green beans, trimmed and halved crosswise

1 stalk celery, trimmed and chopped

1 cup fresh or frozen corn

1 large ripe tomato, chopped

2 Yukon Gold potatoes, chopped

2 bay leaves

1 teaspoon dried basil

2 teaspoons dried oregano

1 cup cooked kidney or garbanzo beans, rinsed and
  drained (see page 11)

2 cups tomato juice

4 cups stock or water

1 cup dried elbow macaroni

Sea salt and freshly ground black pepper

Heat the oil in a large soup pot over high heat. Add the garlic, onion, carrot, green beans, celery, corn, tomato, and potatoes and quick sauté for a few minutes. Add the bay leaves, basil, and oregano and stir. Add the beans, tomato juice, and stock. Cover, bring to a boil, and simmer for approximately 1 hour.

Add the macaroni and simmer for another 5 minutes. Remove the bay leaves and season with salt and pepper. Serve hot.

Traditional Miso Soup

SERVES 4 TO 6

This is an incredibly nutritious soup, thanks to the miso, a fermented soybean paste. There are many varieties of miso. In general, the darker the miso, the stronger the flavor. Experiment with different kinds, as they will all make different tasting soups. Also, remember never to boil miso, which would destroy the live digestive enzymes found in miso.

6 cups stock or water

1 (6-inch) piece wakame, soaked and chopped

1/2 white onion, sliced

1 carrot, thinly sliced on the diagonal

1 (3-inch) piece daikon radish, thinly sliced

2 shiitake mushrooms, stemmed and thinly sliced

2 cups chopped kale or other greens

1/4 cup miso

Fresh watercress or sliced scallion greens for garnish

In a large soup pot, combine the stock and wakame and bring to a boil. Add the onion, carrot, daikon, and mushrooms. Cover and return to a boil. Simmer, covered, for approximately 20 minutes. Add the kale and simmer for another 5 minutes.

Put the miso in a small bowl and dilute it with a little hot soup liquid. Add it to the pot. Gently heat for a couple of minutes or turn the heat off and let the soup steep for 5 to 10 minutes.

Serve the soup in individual bowls and garnish each bowl with the watercress or sliced scallion.

Note: Wakame is a sea vegetable, very rich in minerals. Daikon is a white radish. Both wakame and daikon can be found in health food stores or Asian markets.

66 *The cook and the prophet are one.* 99
    —Murshed Samuel Lewis

Creamy Corn Chowder

SERVES 4 TO 6

This is a favorite at our house. The combination of oats and soy milk gives the soup a creamy consistency, like those cream soups we used to eat. I suggest you use other vegetables, such as broccoli or zucchini, for variations. Be creative.

- 1 to 2 tablespoons canola oil
- 1 yellow onion, diced
- 3 cloves garlic, minced
- 1 carrot, diced
- 1 stalk celery, trimmed and diced
- 4 cups fresh or frozen corn kernals
- 1 russet potato, peeled and diced
- 2 teaspoons dried basil
- 1 tablespoon dried oregano
- 2 tablespoons tamari
- 5 cups stock or water
- 1 cup rolled oats
- 1/4 cup nutritional yeast
- 1 cup soy milk
- Sea salt and freshly ground black pepper

Heat the oil in a large soup pot over medium-high heat. Add the onion, garlic, carrot, celery, corn, and potato and quick sauté for 2 to 3 minutes. Add the basil and oregano and stir. Add the tamari, stock, and oats and stir.

Cover and bring to a boil. Simmer over very low heat for approximately 1 hour. Stir occasionally so the oats do not stick to the bottom of the pot.

Add the nutritional yeast. Stir in the soy milk and heat for a few more minutes. Add salt and pepper and adjust seasonings. Serve hot.

Variation: Substitute 2 zucchinis, trimmed and sliced, for the corn and cook according to the directions above for a delicious Creamy Zucchini Soup.

JOSÉ

I would just like to say that I am very thankful and blessed by the universe to have Rosie come into my life. I have learned so much from her that I don't know where to begin. She has taught me to have more respect for my body, mind, and spirit. I am very grateful to you, Rosie.

As with many people who have helped us, José started out as a customer. He was always appreciative. Years later we were looking for someone to make the sandwiches and José came in with a big smile looking for a job. From Day One he was great, though we often had trouble keeping up with his hair color. He went from black hair to blond to bleached. Perhaps the worst was blue, though we thought he gave Max & Rosie's a little local color. He is a great character, and we miss him since his move to Seattle. He still keeps in touch and we are happy that he is doing fine. Thanks, José. We wish you every happiness.

Gazpacho

SERVES 6 TO 8

Gazpacho is a wonderful cold summer soup that requires no cooking. You can purée some or all of it, but I prefer the crunchy texture of the chopped vegetables.

8 cups tomato juice

6 ripe plum tomatoes, chopped

2 cucumbers, peeled, seeded, and chopped

2 green bell peppers, seeded and chopped

6 scallions, white and green parts, chopped

4 cloves garlic, minced

1/2 cup chopped fresh parsley

1/4 cup chopped fresh basil

1/4 cup freshly squeezed lemon juice

2 tablespoons umeboshi vinegar

Sea salt and freshly ground black pepper

Fresh parsley sprigs or basil leaves for garnish

Combine the tomato juice, tomatoes, cucumbers, bell peppers, scallions, garlic, chopped parsley, chopped basil, lemon juice, and vinegar. Add salt and pepper to taste. Refrigerate for 1 hour.

Serve in individual bowls with a sprig of fresh parsley or a few fresh basil leaves for garnish.

> 66 *Don't cover up the flavor of food with a lot of spices, sauces, and condiments. Let's taste what nature has to offer.* 99
> —Rosie

Navy Bean Soup

SERVES 4 TO 6

If you grew up in the southeastern United States, you probably sampled a navy bean soup quite unlike this one. This is another hearty soup, so if you are having it as a first course, use small bowls!

1 to 2 tablespoons light sesame oil

1 yellow onion, chopped

4 cloves garlic, minced

1 zucchini, cut lengthwise and sliced

1 small rutabaga, peeled and chopped

1 carrot, cut lengthwise and sliced

2 cups cooked navy beans, rinsed and drained (see page 11)

2 tablespoons nutritional yeast

2 teaspoons ground cumin

1 teaspoon dried thyme

Pinch of cayenne pepper

5 cups stock or water

2 tablespoons barley miso

Sea salt and freshly ground black pepper

Heat the oil in a large soup pot over high heat. Add the onion, garlic, zucchini, rutabaga, and carrot and quick sauté for 2 to 3 minutes. Add the beans, nutritional yeast, cumin, thyme, and cayenne pepper and mix. Add the stock. Cover, bring to a boil, and simmer for approximately 1 hour.

In a cup or bowl, dilute the miso in a little hot soup liquid and add it to the pot. Gently heat for a couple of minutes. Add salt and pepper. Adjust the seasonings. Serve hot.

> *Giving up meat reduces the risk of heart disease, stroke, cancer, and many other diseases that cripple and kill millions of Americans annually, and this is not the full story. Change your diet. Do not become one of the statistics.*
> —Max

Split Pea and Garlic Soup

SERVES 4 TO 6

The longer this soup cooks, the thicker and creamier it will get. It's great on the second day, but make sure not to burn it. It usually needs a little more water and a lot of stirring the next day. Serve with a warm baguette. It's Sol's favorite!

1 to 2 tablespoons extra virgin olive oil

1 yellow onion, chopped

8 large cloves garlic, chopped

2 cups green split peas, rinsed

1 carrot, chopped

1 russet potato, peeled and chopped

2 tablespoons tamari

5 cups stock or water

1/4 cup soy milk (optional)

Sea salt and freshly ground black pepper

Heat the oil in a large soup pot over high heat. Add the onion and garlic and quick sauté for 2 to 3 minutes. Add the split peas, carrot, potato, tamari, and stock.

Cover and bring to a boil. Simmer over low heat for approximately 1 hour, stirring occasionally, until the split peas are almost dissolved and the soup is creamy.

Add the soy milk, salt, and pepper, and heat for a few more minutes. Serve hot.

Potato Leek Soup

SERVES 4 TO 6

Puréeing some of the soup with the miso gives this soup a lovely creamy texture. It is light and the slightest bit sweet.

5 cups stock or water

2 bay leaves

4 Yukon Gold potatoes, chopped

1 leek, white and green parts, cut lengthwise and sliced

1 carrot, chopped

2 tablespoons tamari

1 tablespoon dried basil

Pinch of cayenne pepper

3 to 4 tablespoons white miso

Sea salt and freshly ground black pepper

Fresh watercress for garnish

76

In a large soup pot, bring the stock and bay leaves to a boil. Add the potatoes, leek, carrot, tamari, basil, and cayenne pepper. Return to a boil and simmer, covered, for 30 minutes or longer.

Remove 2 cups of the soup and combine in a blender or food processor with the miso. Purée until creamy.

Return to the pot, add salt and pepper, cover, and let sit for 10 minutes. Remove the bay leaves.

Serve in bowls garnished with fresh watercress.

Shiitake Mushroom and Barley Soup

SERVES 4 TO 6

You can use any mushrooms, or a combination of mushrooms, for this soup, although I think it tastes best with shiitakes. If you are not fond of mushrooms, make a vegetable barley soup, substituting 1 cup of your favorite vegetables for the mushrooms.

    1 to 2 tablespoons light sesame oil

    1/2 white onion, chopped

    4 shiitake mushrooms, stemmed and thinly sliced

    1 carrot, chopped

    2 tablespoons tamari

    1/2 cup pearled barley, rinsed

    2 bay leaves

    5 cups stock or water

    Sea salt and freshly ground black pepper

    Sliced scallion greens for garnish

Heat the oil in a large soup pot over high heat. Add the onion and quick sauté for 2 to 3 minutes. Add the mushrooms, carrot, and 1 tablespoon of the tamari. Sauté for a few minutes, until the carrot brightens. Add the barley and the remaining 1 tablespoon of the tamari and stir. Add the bay leaves and stock.

Cover, bring to a boil, and simmer for at least 1 hour.

Add salt and pepper and remove the bay leaves. Serve in individual bowls garnished with sliced scallion.

Garbanzo Cilantro Soup

SERVES 4 TO 6

Try saying this name five times fast! The fresh cilantro mixed with the garbanzo beans produces a wonderful flavor, and the addition of mustard and balsamic vinegar only adds to it. It is filling, as are most bean soups, so small bowls work best.

2 tablespoons extra virgin olive oil

1 yellow onion, chopped

4 cloves garlic, minced

1 carrot, chopped

1 cup finely chopped cilantro, packed

2 Yukon Gold potatoes, chopped

3 cups cooked garbanzo beans, rinsed and drained (see page 11)

5 cups water

1/2 cup tamari

1 tablespoon Dijon mustard

2 tablespoons balsamic vinegar

Sea salt and freshly ground black pepper

Fresh cilantro leaves for garnish

Heat the oil in a large soup pot over high heat. Add the onion, garlic, and carrot, and quick sauté for a few minutes. Add the cilantro, potatoes, and beans and stir. Add the water, tamari, mustard, and vinegar and stir. Cover, bring to a boil, and simmer for approximately 1 hour.

Season with salt and pepper. Serve in individual bowls and garnish with the cilantro leaves.

Menu

Many soups can serve as the main course, with simply a green salad and bread to round out the meal. Miso is not one of those soups. This menu is simple yet tasty, keeping with a macrobiotic theme. Add the parsnips to the chickpeas about 30 minutes before the beans finish cooking. They add a slightly sweet flavor. Steam the collards last so they keep their bright green color. Finish the meal with a cup of Bancha tea. Ah, I'm feeling better already.

Traditional Miso Soup / 69

Sesame Stir-Fry over Brown Rice / 26

Chickpeas / 11
with Chopped Parsnips

Steamed Collard Greens with
Lemon Tahini Dressing / 96

Class 6: Sensational Salads

Café Max & Rosie's

80

Part I: Rosie's
Cooking Classes

Sensational Salads

AN INTRODUCTION TO SALADS

Fresh vegetable salads are delightful to eat in the warm weather, when organic and locally grown produce is readily available and beautifully fresh. This is also the time when we need to eat cooling foods.

Salads need not be dull or repetitious. Try using some beautiful garnishes, like edible flowers and fresh herbs. Seeds, such as pumpkin or sunflower, are great as well, and add protein to the salad. Fresh bean sprouts are good for their crunchy texture as well as their protein content. I often add tempeh "croutons" to my salads for the added protein as well as the taste.

Use lots of greens in your salads, not just lettuce. Baby mixed greens or mesclun are readily available and all you have to do is put some in your bowl. Arugula (my favorite green) mixed with lettuce or baby spinach leaves gives a bite to the salad. I don't recommend using iceberg lettuce because it has very little nutritional value and very little color! In addition to the greens, use different colored vegetables to make a visual masterpiece.

You will need to wash the vegetables carefully, especially the leafy greens, which can sometimes have a lot of dirt on the inner leaves. If you are not using organic vegetables, make sure to wash them thoroughly. You can also use a liquid vegetable cleaner to soak them in, which may help to remove some of the pesticides. Liquid vegetable cleaner is a natural wash for fruits and vegetables that helps remove pesticides, chemicals, wax, dirt, and inorganic pollutants. Mix it with water and soak your vegetables and fruits. It can be found at most supermarkets and health food stores.

In addition to fresh vegetable salads, you can make delicious grain, bean, or pasta salads and serve them as a complete meal. Leftover grains and beans are perfect for this. And remember, the same salad with a different dressing and garnishes is a new meal in itself. Again, it's a great opportunity to be creative. So let's make some sensational salads.

Fresh-from-the-Garden Salad

SERVES 4 TO 6

This mixed vegetable salad works well with just about any dressing, but serve the dressing on the side so that it doesn't affect the presentation of the beautiful, brightly colored vegetables.

1 head fresh red leaf lettuce, torn

8 to 10 ounces fresh arugula, whole leaves

1 large tomato, halved and sliced

1 cucumber, peeled and thinly sliced

1 carrot, peeled and shredded

1/4 red cabbage, shredded

1/4 pound fresh mushrooms, trimmed and sliced

1 cup broccoli florets

2 cups clover sprouts

Hulled sunflower seeds for garnish

Place the lettuce and arugula in a large salad bowl or platter. Add the tomato, cucumber, carrot, cabbage, mushrooms, and broccoli so the pieces are spread out and the colors well mixed. Garnish with clover sprouts and a sprinkle of sunflower seeds. Serve with your favorite dressing on the side.

" *There's nothing like picking fresh vegetables from the garden for dinner. Their sweet freshness actually speaks to you. Listen.* "
—*Rosie*

JEFF, AKA "CHEF JEFF"

Max & Rosie's is a great place to work. You get to meet a great melting pot of people. The atmosphere is fun and energetic. I take pride in serving fresh, quality food. I cook and serve for people as I would want to be served. Besides, lots of pretty women come in to see why I was voted "Asheville's Local Sex Symbol, 1999 and 2000."

And then there is Jeff, Rosie's brother. Rosie's parents are very family oriented and their son, Jeff, who worked the coffee shops with Sol for 15 years, was still living in Florida. It was time for Max to go back to his painting and, miraculously, Jeff was ready to come to Asheville. Having seen many people work the sandwich board, we must say, Jeff is the best. He has a fine relationship with his dad. He really is a chip off the old block, a man capable of flirting with a pretty woman while making a fabulous sandwich, never missing a beat. Rosie often speaks of how much she enjoys working with him. No matter how busy it is, he manages to stay relaxed and keep a smile on his face, while getting the food out with incredible speed. We are very grateful to have him here.

Rhia Me Dear Brown Rice and Avocado Salad

SERVES 4

Rhia me dear, she is so dear. A friend of Dana's, so I hear. Who ever thought she'd end up on a plate!

1 head fresh green leaf lettuce, torn

6 cups cooked brown rice (see page 24)

2 large tomatoes, cut in wedges

1 cucumber, peeled and sliced

1 carrot, peeled and shredded

5 ounces fresh alfalfa sprouts

2 avocados, sliced

Unhulled sesame seeds for garnish

Rosie's World-Famous Tangy Tofu Dressing (see page 121)

Place one-quarter of the leaf lettuce on a plate and put a 1^1/$_2$-cup mound of the warm rice in the center. Surround the rice with a quarter of the tomatoes, cucumber, shredded carrot, and sprouts, and whatever else you like that is in season. Arrange one-quarter of the sliced avocado on the rice and sprinkle with sesame seeds. Repeat with the remaining ingredients to make 4 plates. Serve immediately with the dressing on the side.

" *Earth laughs in flowers.* "
—*Ralph Waldo Emerson*

Fresh Spinach and Feta Salad

SERVES 4

If the spinach isn't prewashed, wash it well because it usually has a lot of dirt in it. If you can get baby spinach, it works well for this salad, as it has a little sweeter flavor than mature spinach. Serve the salad with some crusty bread or warmed pitas.

1 pound fresh spinach leaves

1 large tomato, cut in wedges

1 cucumber, peeled and sliced

1 red onion, thinly sliced

8 canned artichoke hearts, halved (optional)

2 cups mixed crunchy sprouts

1 cup crumbled feta cheese

Kalamata olives for garnish

Lemon Vinaigrette Dressing (see page 97)

Divide the spinach among 4 plates. Arrange the tomato, cucumber, onion, artichokes, and sprouts on top of the spinach. Sprinkle the feta over the salads. Garnish with the olives. Pass the dressing at the table.

Mediterranean Salad

SERVES 4 TO 6

A light, colorful salad that goes great with any meal. It is high in protein as well.

Light sesame oil for frying

4 ounces soy tempeh, cubed

Sea salt

1 head curly leaf lettuce, red or green, torn

1 cucumber, peeled and sliced

4 to 6 red radishes, trimmed and thinly sliced

1 stalk celery, cut on the diagonal

1 tomato, cut in chunks

1/2 pound button mushrooms, trimmed and thinly sliced

1/2 cup toasted pumpkin seeds for garnish

8 to 10 black olives for garnish

Ume-Balsamic Dressing (see page 97)

**Part I: Rosie's
Cooking Classes**

Heat about 1/2 inch of oil in a cast-iron skillet over high heat. Add the tempeh and deep fry until crispy and golden on all sides. Salt lightly, drain on paper towels, and set aside.

Place the lettuce in the bottom of a large salad bowl and add the cucumber, radishes, celery, tomato, and mushrooms, arranging them according to color. Top with the tempeh cubes. Garnish with the seeds and olives. Pour the dressing over the salad just before serving and toss gently.

Spring Mix with Tempeh Croutons

<u>SERVES 4 TO 6</u>

Mesclun is a mixture of several kinds of salad greens, especially baby lettuce. Often the greens are prewashed and ready to use for salads. I buy mesclun under the name of "spring mix." It is usually a nice assortment of lettuce, frisée, radicchio, arugula, and other leafy greens.

$1/4$ cup tamari

1 teaspoon granulated garlic

1 teaspoon freshly squeezed ginger juice (see page 5)

1 (8-ounce) piece soy tempeh, cubed

Light sesame oil for frying

1 pound mesclun

2 Jerusalem artichokes, peeled and sliced

4 red radishes, trimmed and sliced

1 cucumber, peeled and sliced

1 yellow bell pepper, thinly sliced

2 plum tomatoes, sliced

Lemon Basil Dressing (see page 101)

In a small bowl, mix the tamari, garlic, and ginger juice. Sprinkle the mixture over the tempeh. Heat about $1/2$ inch of oil in a cast-iron skillet over high heat. Add the tempeh and deep fry until crispy on all sides. Drain on paper towels and set aside.

Place the mesclun in a large salad bowl. Arrange the Jerusalem artichokes, radishes, cucumber, bell pepper, and tomatoes on top of the greens so that they are visually pleasing. Top with the tempeh croutons. Serve at once, passing the dressing at the table.

Quinoa–Black Bean Salad

This salad makes a great lunch and can also be used as a small side with a sandwich, instead of potato salad or pasta salad. I prefer it at room temperature rather than cold. If you do refrigerate the salad, make sure it is tightly covered so that it doesn't dry out.

1 cup quinoa, rinsed

2 cups water

2 cups cooked black beans, rinsed and drained (see page 11)

2 cups fresh or frozen corn, cooked and drained

1 small red onion, chopped

2 plum tomatoes, chopped

1 cup packed chopped fresh cilantro

1 ripe avocado, cut into 1/2-inch cubes

Leaf lettuce

Sliced black olives for garnish

Lemon wedges for garnish

Dressing

1/4 cup extra virgin olive oil

2 tablespoons balsamic vinegar

2 tablespoons freshly squeezed lime juice

2 cloves garlic, minced

2 tablespoons nutritional yeast

2 teaspoons ground cumin

Sea salt and freshly ground black pepper

Combine the quinoa and water and cook according to the Grain Cooking Chart (see page 24).

In a large bowl, mix the beans with the corn and onion. Add the tomatoes and cilantro.

In a small bowl, make the dressing by combining the oil, vinegar, lime juice, garlic, nutritional yeast, cumin, and salt and pepper. Mix well and set aside.

When the quinoa is cooked, remove it from the pot, place it in a bowl, and stir so it cools. Let it sit for about 15 minutes, and then add the quinoa and dressing to the large bowl and toss. Let stand at room temperature for 1 hour (if you have the time) for the flavors to blend.

Add the avocado and mix. Serve on a bed of leaf lettuce with a garnish of black olives and lemon wedges.

Vegetable Pasta Salad

SERVES 4 TO 6

This salad is one of my family's favorites, especially in the warmer weather. It requires some cooking, but it is a filling meal in itself. I usually use penne, but occasionally I use shells. The dressing is creamy, and you may want to make some extra to keep on the table for those who can't seem to get enough. Edible flowers add to the beauty.

1 pound penne or shell pasta

1 pound asparagus, trimmed and sliced on the diagonal

3 to 5 tablespoons extra virgin olive oil

1 large portobello mushroom, trimmed and sliced

2 tablespoons balsamic vinegar

1 (8-ounce) piece soy tempeh, cubed (optional)

Sea salt

1/2 head fresh red leaf lettuce, torn

10 to 12 ounces fresh spinach, trimmed and torn

10 to 12 ounces fresh arugula, trimmed and torn

Handful fresh basil leaves

1 red bell pepper, seeded and thinly sliced

Handful walnuts for garnish

Edible flowers for garnish (optional)

Dressing

1/2 cup Nayonnaise

1/2 to 3/4 cup extra virgin olive oil

2 tablespoons balsamic vinegar

1 tablespoon umeboshi vinegar

3 tablespoons water

1/2 teaspoon granulated garlic

2 tablespoons nutritional yeast

Cook the pasta according to the package directions. Drain, rinse under cold water, and set aside in the pot with cold water to cover. This will keep it from sticking.

Steam the asparagus for 5 to 8 minutes, until bright green and still crispy. Remove from the steamer and set aside to cool.

Heat 1 to 2 tablespoons of the oil in a cast-iron skillet over high heat. Add the mushroom and balsamic vinegar and sauté for about 2 minutes. Remove from the pan and set aside to cool.

Add the remaining 2 to 3 tablespoons of oil to the skillet. Add the tempeh and fry for 8 to 10 minutes, turning frequently, until crispy and golden. Salt lightly, drain on paper towels, and set aside.

Combine the lettuce, spinach, and arugula in a large serving bowl and toss. Add the fresh basil leaves. Drain the pasta and add it to the salad.

To make the dressing, combine the Nayonnaise, oil, vinegars, water, garlic, and nutritional yeast in a bowl. Blend with a whisk until smooth.

Add the dressing to the pasta salad and toss well. Top with the red pepper, asparagus, portobello mushroom, and tempeh cubes. Garnish with the walnuts and edible flowers. Serve at room temperature.

Garbanzo Bean and Tomato Salad

SERVES 4 TO 6

This is a tasty salad that I usually serve in the summer. I like to eat it with brown rice or couscous mixed in, or as a side dish with a green salad and whole-grain bread. I like a lot of freshly ground black pepper in this salad. As I suggested earlier, beans should be served with whole grains and in small quantities.

6 cups cooked garbanzo beans, rinsed and drained (see page 11)

4 ripe plum tomatoes, chopped

1 red onion, chopped

1 cup coarsely chopped fresh cilantro

4 cloves garlic, minced

1 tablespoon balsamic vinegar

$1/4$ to $1/2$ cup extra virgin olive oil

Sea salt and freshly ground black pepper

Leaf lettuce or mixed greens

In a large bowl, combine the beans, tomatoes, onion, cilantro, garlic, vinegar, oil, and salt and pepper. Let sit for at least 1 hour at room temperature or in the refrigerator to allow the flavors to blend.

Serve on a bed of leaf lettuce or mixed greens.

Menu

This menu is nice served for lunch or as a light dinner in spring or summer. It does not require much cooking, but there is a good deal of vegetable chopping. The light coolness of the gazpacho goes well with the heartier pasta salad.

Gazpacho / 73

Vegetable Pasta Salad / 90

Warm Baguette

Class 7: Delicious Dressings, Dips, and a Gravy

Café Max & Rosie's

94

Part I: Rosie's
Cooking Classes

Delicious Dressings, Dips, and a Gravy

AN INTRODUCTION TO DRESSINGS, DIPS, AND A GRAVY

The taste of salad dressings is very important; oftentimes, they make the salad. You want them to be delicious but not overpowering.

The dressings and dips that follow are extremely tasty. All the recipes should be adjusted to your individual taste. Some are pretty strongly flavored, like the Green Garlic Dip and Horseradish Mustard Dressing. If the flavors are too strong for you, tone them down by simply decreasing the amount of garlic or horseradish you use. Remember when tasting, however, that the flavors will tone down when the dressings are tossed with a salad or used as a dip for vegetables or crackers. So try them as is first, and then if you need to adjust them, go right ahead. All leftover dressings must be refrigerated, and will keep 5 to 7 days.

For most of these recipes you will need a food processor or blender; but for some, you can use a whisk or shaker to mix the ingredients.

Class 7:
Dressings, Dips,
and a Gravy

Lemon Tahini Dressing

Compared to the Garlic Tahini Dressing below, this dressing is more lemony and the other more garlicky, as the names suggest. Use them interchangeably. They're both great as a salad dressing, as a sauce on baked potatoes or tempeh, or on any grain. You can also use them as a dip for fresh vegetables.

1 cup tahini

1/2 cup water

1/4 to 1/2 cup freshly squeezed lemon juice

2 tablespoons tamari

Pinch of cayenne pepper

Combine all the ingredients in a blender or food processor and blend until creamy. Refrigerate before serving.

Garlic Tahini Dressing

MAKES ABOUT 2 CUPS

At Café Max & Rosie's we use this dressing for our falafel pitas as well as for salad dressing. Adjust the garlic to your taste.

1 1/4 cups tahini

1/2 cup water

2 tablespoons tamari

2 cloves garlic, pressed

1/2 teaspoon ground cumin

Combine all the ingredients in a blender or food processor and blend until creamy. Refrigerate before serving.

Ume-Balsamic Dressing

MAKES ABOUT 1 CUP

My family has been using this dressing for about ten years, on almost every salad we eat for dinner, and no one has tired of it yet. As a matter of fact, we all crave it. It is a simple dressing, but so tasty. Toss with a green or mixed salad and let the salad sit for a few minutes at room temperature before serving.

2/3 cup extra virgin olive oil

2 tablespoons balsamic vinegar

2 tablespoons water

3 tablespoons umeboshi vinegar

1 clove garlic, minced

4 tablespoons nutritional yeast

Blend all the ingredients. Shaking in a container works fine for this.

Lemon Vinaigrette Dressing

MAKES ABOUT 2 CUPS

This is a pretty standard dressing at Max & Rosie's. Although we call it a vinaigrette, it actually doesn't contain any vinegar. Some of our customers call it "Lemon Dijon Dressing."

1/4 cup extra virgin olive oil

1/2 cup canola oil

3/4 cup freshly squeezed lemon juice

1/2 cup tamari

2 tablespoons stone-ground mustard

Blend all the ingredients. Shaking in a container works fine for this. Refrigerate before serving.

> *When you say thanks at mealtime, really feel that*
> *gratefulness. We are the minority who can leave*
> *the table with a full belly.*
> —Rosie

Tofu-Tahini Dip

MAKES ABOUT 2 CUPS

This is a nice, thick dip for tahini lovers. Use it as a dip for vegetables or crackers, or as a sandwich spread.

8 ounces firm tofu

$1/2$ cup tahini

2 tablespoons tamari

2 tablespoons freshly squeezed lemon juice

$1/2$ teaspoon honey

2 tablespoons nutritional yeast

2 tablespoons unhulled sesame seeds for garnish

Combine the tofu, tahini, tamari, lemon juice, honey, and nutritional yeast in a blender or food processor and blend until creamy. Transfer to a serving bowl, garnish with the sesame seeds, and refrigerate for 30 minutes before serving.

> *Our purpose as humans is not merely survival; rather it*
> *is to experience life intensely, to bless and be blessed by*
> *this opportunity called life.*
> —Max

Green Garlic Dip or Dressing

MAKES 1 1/2 CUPS

This dip has a strong garlic flavor, so if it's too strong, decrease the amount of garlic. I prefer it with fresh basil, but the parsley works just as well. Serve it as a dip with fresh vegetables or crackers. It can also be used as a sauce for grains or pastas or a dressing for salads.

- 4 ounces silken tofu
- 6 cloves garlic, minced
- 1 cup tightly packed fresh basil or parsley
- 1/4 cup chopped onion
- 1 cup extra virgin olive oil
- 3 tablespoons balsamic vinegar
- Sea salt and freshly ground black pepper

Combine all the ingredients in a blender or food processor and blend until creamy. Refrigerate the mixture if you are using it as a dip, and it will thicken a bit more. If it is too thick, add a small amount of water. Let the mixture sit at room temperature if you are serving it as a sauce on cooked vegetables, grains, or pasta.

Café Max & Rosie's

100

Part I: Rosie's
Cooking Classes

Horseradish Mustard Dressing

This is a hot one, so adjust the flavor to your liking. Aside from its use as a salad dressing, it is great as a dip or on sandwiches. At Max & Rosie's it is often requested "on the side."

  1 cup prepared horseradish

  4 teaspoons freshly squeezed lemon juice

  1/4 cup stone-ground mustard

  3/4 cup Nayonnaise

  1 teaspoon sea salt (optional)

  2 teaspoons freshly ground black pepper (optional)

Whisk all the ingredients in a bowl. Refrigerate before serving.

Lemon Basil Dressing

MAKES ABOUT 1 CUP

The combination of lemon and fresh basil gives this dressing a refreshingly springlike flavor, and I tend to use it more often in the warmer weather.

  2/3 cup extra virgin olive oil

  1/2 cup freshly squeezed lemon juice

  2 cloves garlic, minced

  1 cup fresh basil, chopped

  Sea salt and freshly ground black pepper

Combine all the ingredients in a blender or food processor and blend until creamy. Refrigerate before serving.

DI (DIANA)

I first visited Asheville in the midst of a blizzard. It was December, 1993, and given my hatred of cold weather, it's a wonder I ever returned. But the first hearth I crossed was such a warm and friendly one—Café Max & Rosie's—that I was enticed back.

It wasn't just the great juices and vegetarian food; it was the company. Here were two people I liked right away. It was a social occasion for me, to perch myself up at the counter, and in between Max's and Rosie's busy activities, we would chat and get acquainted.

The café is a melting pot of sorts. It draws the most interesting characters of Asheville, as well as the more conservative of the community. When I first started working at the café on Sundays, there were nights when I just could not close at the appointed time because people didn't want to leave.

Having been on both sides of the counter, I know how much hard work and love go into preparing the food and keeping the customers happy, and that is just what happens at Max & Rosie's. I'm glad to see that the recipes will now find a wider audience than those lucky few who stumble upon the café in Asheville.

At Max & Rosie's we have guests from all over the world who, like Di, have popped in, eaten, and become part of our lives. A native of Australia and a self-described world traveler, she is an attractive, bubbly person who rapidly moves toward the center of any scene. Shortly after moving from New York to Asheville, she made us an offer we could not refuse. She wanted to have a Psychic Fair at Max & Rosie's on Sundays. With an enthusiasm that is hard to resist, the project was launched, and it was a delight seeing Di's charming friendliness at work. From small beginnings, we now have three psychics at work, and Max & Rosie's is the place to come to be well nourished and psychically advised. Di has certainly been one of the Max & Rosie's angels. The travels of Di continue, and we have just had a postcard from Spain, reporting much calamitous carryings on. We are sure that the karmic connection with Di is not over and we expect to see her soon.

Class 7:
Dressings, Dips,
and a Gravy

Mushroom Gravy

MAKES ABOUT 3 CUPS

This gravy goes great on just about everything, from whole grains to tofu to vegetables to mashed potatoes. It has become a tradition at our house to have this gravy on Thanksgiving with "tofu turkey." You can substitute shiitake or portobello mushrooms for the button mushrooms if you like.

1 to 2 tablespoons light sesame oil

1/2 yellow onion, chopped

2 cloves garlic, minced

1/2 pound button mushrooms, trimmed and thinly sliced

2 1/2 cups soy milk

1/4 cup tamari

3 tablespoons arrowroot or kuzu

1/4 cup cold water

Sea salt and freshly ground black pepper

Heat the oil in a small saucepan over medium-high heat. Add the onion, garlic, and mushrooms and sauté for 8 to 10 minutes, until the onion is translucent. Add the soy milk and tamari and lower the heat. Stir. Bring the heat back up until the gravy begins to bubble.

Dissolve the arrowroot in the water. While stirring, add the mixture to the saucepan. Continue to stir for a minute or two, until the gravy is thick. If it is not thick enough, dissolve a little more arrowroot in a small amount of cold water and slowly add it to the gravy, while stirring. Season with salt and pepper. Serve hot.

Menu

In this menu, the portobello mushroom caps can be served as an appetizer or as a side dish. Spread the Green Garlic Dressing on the caps and bake for about 30 minutes at 350°. If the dressing dries out, spread more dressing on before serving. The cucumber in the spring mix and the light salad dressing cools down the mushrooms.

Creamy Corn Chowder / 70

Vegetable Medley over Basmati Rice / 27

Baked Portobello Mushroom Caps
with Green Garlic Dressing / 100

Mesclun with Cucumber Slices
with Lemon Vinaigrette Dressing / 97

Class 8: The World's Best Vegetarian Sandwiches (And Some Great Pitas, Too!)

Café Max & Rosie's

106

Part I: Rosie's
Cooking Classes

Vegetarian Sandwiches

AN INTRODUCTION TO SANDWICH MAKING

Café Max & Rosie's is perhaps best known for our incredibly tasty vegetarian sandwiches.

You may not think there's much to making a vegetarian sandwich but, believe me, it is an art like any other aspect of cooking. The creativity comes in combining different tastes and textures that blend together, yet stand out individually.

In the summertime many of our customers are tourists, some of whom have no idea that Max & Rosie's is a vegetarian café. Although a few do leave after looking at the menu (do you have hamburgers?), most stay and try something they are totally unaccustomed to, and are surprised at how much they enjoy it!

Many of our sandwiches take their inspiration from a traditional meat sandwich, such as a BLT or a Reuben. Tofu and tempeh are perfect foods to use for this purpose, as you can season them to taste any way you would like, and they have a sort of meatlike consistency. We take out the meat and put in the soy, eliminate the cholesterol, lower the fat, and keep it extremely tasty. I prefer to prepare all the sandwiches vegan. If you prefer cow's milk cheese to soy cheese, feel free to substitute.

Pita sandwiches are usually light and filled with lots of vegetables. They taste best if the pitas have been slightly warmed first. To warm them, you can place the whole pita in a small paper bag and put in a warm oven (250°) for approximately 5 minutes. If you leave them in too long, they will get hard. Another method is to steam them in a vegetable steamer for less than a minute. If you steam them too long, they will become soggy. If the pita is small, just cut off the top before filling. If it is large, you can cut it in half for two. We use whole wheat pitas at the café, but they do come in several varieties, so you may want to try some others.

All of the sandwich recipes yield four sandwiches, so if you're just making yourself a sandwich, simply divide the recipe by four.

And now for some of those world-renowned sandwiches for you to try at home and enjoy. We'll tell you the ingredients, you put them together!

Tofu or Tempeh Reuben

SERVES 4

Remember those big, fatty corned beef reubens that are guaranteed to clog your arteries? We've created a low-fat, cholesterol-free version that will tantalize your taste buds.

1 pound firm tofu, sliced lengthwise into 4 pieces or 1 (8-ounce) piece tempeh, cut in half and sliced lengthwise into 4 pieces

1/2 cup tamari

6 to 8 tablespoons canola oil

Stone-ground mustard

8 slices rye bread

8 slices Swiss-style soy cheese

4 slices tomato

1 cup packed sauerkraut

Put the tofu on a plate and cover with the tamari. Turn until coated on both sides. Heat the oil in a large cast-iron skillet over high heat. Add the tofu, reserving the leftover tamari for another dish. Fry the tofu for 5 minutes on each side, turning once, until browned. Remove the tofu from the skillet and place on paper towels to remove some of the oil.

Spread the mustard on the bread. Put 1 piece of soy cheese on each slice, then add the tofu, tomato, and sauerkraut. Close the sandwich.

Place the sandwich in the same skillet over medium heat with a weight on the sandwich. (A heavy plate will do fine.) Cook for 2 to 3 minutes, until it begins to brown, then turn the sandwich over. Cook 2 to 3 minutes on the other side, until crispy on the bottom. Cut the sandwich in half and serve immediately.

Club TLT

SERVES 4

Remember those BLTs you ate years ago? Well, this is a vegetarian version. It's a triple-decker delight!

2 (8-ounce) pieces tempeh, cut in half and sliced lengthwise
   into 8 pieces

$^1/_2$ cup tamari

6 to 8 tablespoons canola oil

12 slices whole-grain bread, toasted

Nayonnaise

8 lettuce leaves

8 slices tomato

5 ounces alfalfa sprouts, divided into eight bunches

Place the tempeh on a plate and cover with the tamari. Turn until coated on both sides.

Heat the oil in a large cast-iron skillet over high heat. Add the tempeh, reserving the tamari for another dish. Fry the tempeh for 5 minutes on each side, turning once, until browned on both sides.

Layer the sandwich as follows: On a piece of toast, spread the Nayonnaise, then add 1 piece of lettuce, 1 slice of tempeh, 1 slice of tomato, and one bunch of sprouts. Repeat the layers on the second piece of toast. Top with the third slice of toast and carefully cut the sandwich in half. It works best to hold it together with club toothpicks, as this is a big one!

Class 8:
Sandwiches

SWAMI VIRATO

Eating at Max & Rosie's goes beyond mere food.
As Japanese culture has shown, how we eat—the
ambiance—is as important as the food itself. Eating
at Max & Rosie's is an experience of love as much
as it is a culinary delight. I also love the smoothies
they offer, especially their tantric smoothies....

Although Swami Virato was not employed at Max & Rosie's, we thought his was a story to include. About six years ago Swami, a rather wild looking man in his midlife, came into the café. You have probably read his magazine, *New Frontier*, which is now on the Internet. From the beginning, he was a good friend. He asked us if we would be prepared to have Steven Halpern play in the café. (We have, by the way, a magnificent grand piano in the café.) The thought of having the famous Steven Halpern play at Max & Rosie's was delightful! We had long enjoyed his music. We thought the intimate setting (aside from the noise of the restaurant equipment) was a perfect setting for Steven's music. The concert was a great success, and we offer our heartfelt thanks to Steven and Swami for so generously allowing it to happen. Steven still talks about the time he did a free concert at a "Jewish vegetarian delicatessen."

Tempeh "Steak" Sandwich

SERVES 4

This recipe and the variation that follows are incredibly delicious. There are many possibilities for tempeh sandwich variations just by using a sauce, such as barbecue or Thai. Use your imagination and see what you come up with.

1 (8-ounce) piece tempeh, cut in half and sliced lengthwise
    into 4 pieces

1/2 cup tamari

6 to 8 tablespoons safflower oil

1 onion, sliced

12 button mushrooms, trimmed and sliced

8 slices sourdough bread

Horseradish Mustard Dressing (see page 101)

4 slices mozzarella-style soy cheese

Place the tempeh on a plate and cover with the tamari. Turn until coated on both sides.

Heat the oil in a large cast-iron skillet over high heat. Add the tempeh, reserving the tamari for another dish. Fry the tempeh for 5 minutes on each side, turning once, until browned on both sides. Remove the tempeh from the skillet and add the onion and mushrooms. Sauté for 5 to 8 minutes, until the onion is translucent.

Lightly toast the bread, spread the dressing on it, and add the tempeh, soy cheese, onion, and mushrooms. Close the sandwich and carefully cut it in half. Serve immediately.

Variation on the Tempeh Sandwich Theme

There are many different tempeh sandwiches just waiting to be created. The artichoke hearts and dressing in this one make it a winner!

1 (8-ounce) piece tempeh, cut in half and sliced lengthwise into 4 pieces

^{1}/2 cup tamari

6 to 8 tablespoons light sesame oil

Rosie's World-Famous Tangy Tofu Dressing (see page 121)

1 loaf whole-grain French bread, cut in four and sliced in half

4 slices cheddar-style or mozzarella-style soy cheese

8 canned artichoke hearts, sliced

4 slices tomato

Place the tempeh on a plate and cover with the tamari. Turn until coated on both sides.

Heat the oil in a large cast-iron skillet over high heat. Add the tempeh, reserving the tamari for another dish. Fry the tempeh for 5 minutes on each side, turning once, until browned on both sides.

Spread the dressing on the bread, then add the tempeh, soy cheese, artichoke hearts, and tomato. Close the sandwich and heat it over medium heat in the covered skillet for a couple of minutes. Cut in half and serve warm.

Tofu Supreme

SERVES 4

This high-protein sandwich is one of our most popular "daily specials" at Café Max & Rosie's. The avocado adds a great flavor.

1 pound firm tofu, sliced lengthwise into 4 pieces

$1/2$ cup tamari

6 to 8 tablespoons canola oil

1 loaf whole-grain French bread, cut in four and sliced in half

Nayonnaise

4 slices mozzarella-style soy cheese

2 ripe avocados, sliced

4 slices tomato

4 slices red onion

5 ounces alfalfa or clover sprouts

Place the tofu on a plate and cover with the tamari. Turn until coated on both sides.

Heat the oil in a large cast-iron skillet over high heat. Add the tofu, reserving the tamari for another dish. Fry the tofu for 3 to 5 minutes on each side, turning once, until browned on both sides.

Warm the bread in a 250° oven for 2 to 3 minutes. Spread the Nayonnaise on the bread and place the tofu, soy cheese, avocado, tomato, red onion, and sprouts on top. Close the sandwich and cut in half. Serve warm.

Tantalizing Tofu Classic

SERVES 4

The combination of fried tofu and horseradish is great tasting. I suggest adding the optional avocado slices, as it cools down the flavor of the dressing.

1 pound firm tofu, sliced lengthwise into 4 pieces

1/2 cup tamari

6 to 8 tablespoons light sesame oil

Horseradish Mustard Dressing (see page 101)

8 slices sourdough bread, toasted

4 leaves green lettuce

4 slices tomato

4 slices red onion

2 ripe avocados, sliced (optional)

5 ounces alfalfa sprouts

Place the tofu on a plate and cover with the tamari. Turn the tofu until coated on all sides.

Heat the oil in a large cast-iron skillet over high heat. Add the tofu, reserving the tamari for another dish. Fry the tofu for 3 to 5 minutes on each side, turning once, until browned on both sides.

Spread a small amount (because it is spicy) of the dressing on the bread (you can always add more). Place the lettuce, tofu, tomato, red onion, avocado, and sprouts on the bread and close the sandwich. Cut in half and serve.

Part I: Rosie's Cooking Classes

Café Max & Rosie's

Hummus Pita

SERVES 4

Hummus is traditionally served in a pita. It's also good as a dip with pita crisps.

4 cups packed shredded lettuce

4 whole-wheat pitas, warmed

4 cups Hummus (see page 15)

4 to 8 slices tomato

4 slices red onion (optional)

Alfalfa sprouts

Rosie's World-Famous Tangy Tofu Dressing (see page 121)

Place lettuce in the bottom of each pita. Add a generous portion of hummus surrounded by tomato, onion, and sprouts. Top with a dollop of the dressing and serve.

Class 8:
Sandwiches

66 *What really gets me are the meat restaurant billboards,*
like the one that has the cute, fat pig smiling and dancing.
Is this how a pig acts on its way to the slaughterhouse?
I don't think so. But what kind of picture does it provide
for the children? 99
—Rosie

Vegan Veggie Pita

SERVES 4

This is basically a salad in a pita. You can add grilled tofu, tempeh, or soy cheese for the extra protein (and flavor). Also, try it with fresh avocado slices. Yum.

4 cups packed shredded leaf lettuce

4 whole-wheat pitas, warmed

4 slices tomato

2 cups shredded carrots

16 slices cucumber

12 to 16 broccoli florets

8 button mushrooms, trimmed and sliced

Rosie's World-Famous Tangy Tofu Dressing (see page 121)

Sprouts for topping

Place lettuce in the bottom of each pita, then layer the vegetables alternating with the dressing. Use as much or as little dressing as you like. Top the pita with more dressing and sprouts. Serve at once.

 What is hateful to you, do not do to your fellowman. That is the entire Law. All the rest is commentary.
—The Talmud

Mideast Bean Pita

SERVES 4

This pita requires a little cooking first. The bulgur mixture can also be served warm on a plate. At the café we serve it with falafel balls, salad, and pita bread on the side.

1 cup bulgur

2 cups water

1 cup cooked garbanzo beans, rinsed and drained (see page 11)

4 cloves garlic, minced

2 tablespoons freshly squeezed lemon juice

2 tablespoons extra virgin olive oil

Sea salt and freshly ground black pepper

1/2 cup chopped fresh parsley

4 whole-wheat pitas, warmed

4 cups packed shredded lettuce

4 slices tomato

12 cucumber slices

Clover sprouts

Garlic Tahini Dressing (see page 96)

Combine the bulgur and water in a pot and cook according to the Grain Cooking Chart (see page 24). Transfer to a bowl and add the garbanzo beans, garlic, lemon juice, olive oil, and salt and pepper. Mix. When cool, mix in the parsley.

Stuff each pita with the lettuce on the bottom, then the bulgur mixture, surrounded by tomato and cucumber slices. Top with sprouts and the dressing and serve at once.

Menu

I am not one to serve sandwiches for dinner, so this is strictly a lunch menu for me. At the café we serve our sandwiches with chips (potato or corn) and a pickle. Sandwiches are also nice to serve with a tossed salad, or try them with the Quinoa–Black Bean Salad (see page 88). Of course, there's also the traditional potato salad, cole slaw, or macaroni salad.

Club TLT / 109

**Corn Chips
and Jericho Salsa / 130**

Sliced Cucumbers and Carrots

Class 9: Max & Rosie's Top-Secret Recipes

120

These are the recipes that customers have begged for, offered money for, and desperately tried to make themselves. Well, we promised they'd be included. And here they are!

Top-Secret Recipes!

Rosie's World-Famous Tangy Tofu Dressing

MAKES ABOUT 4 CUPS

This is the most frequently requested recipe at Max & Rosie's. The recipe is simple but the secret is to follow it exactly, *as some people I've given the recipe to (like my mom) just can't seem to get it right! You can, however, experiment with the tofu, using soft or even silken for a thinner dressing, or extra firm for a thicker dip.*

1 pound firm tofu

1/2 cup freshly squeezed lemon juice

1/2 cup tamari

1/2 cup tahini

1/2 cup canola oil

4 teaspoons granulated garlic

1/2 cup packed chopped fresh parsley

Combine all the ingredients in a food processor or blender and blend until creamy. Use immediately or store covered in a refrigerator for up to 5 days.

66 *Our bodies are our gardens,*

to which our wills are gardeners. 99

—*William Shakespeare*

Fried Rice Ch'Poppi

SERVES 4

This recipe is named for Sol, Rosie's dad, whom the grandchildren call "Poppi." It is good for lunch or dinner, served with a salad or corn chips and salsa. If you have leftover rice and black beans, it takes no time at all to prepare.

2 to 3 tablespoons canola oil

4 cloves garlic, chopped

2 stalks celery, chopped

1 carrot, chopped

1 cup fresh or frozen corn

2 cups cooked black beans, rinsed and drained (see page 11)

4 cups cooked brown rice (see page 24)

2 tablespoons tamari

Freshly ground black pepper

4 (8-inch) flour tortillas

Garlic Tahini Dressing (see page 96) or Lemon Tahini Dressing (see page 96)

Sliced black olives for garnish

Heat the oil in a large cast-iron skillet over medium-high heat. Add the garlic, celery, carrot, and corn and sauté for 5 to 10 minutes, until the vegetables are tender but not mushy. Mix the black beans and rice with the tamari and add to the vegetables. Add black pepper.

Preheat the oven to 350°.

Place the tortillas on a work surface, divide the mixture into 4 equal servings, and place a portion down the middle of each tortilla.

Transfer the tortillas to a lightly oiled cookie sheet. Spoon on a little dressing, enough to cover the length of the tortillas. Fold the tortillas and top with more sauce.

Bake for approximately 15 minutes, until the tortillas begin to brown.

Garnish with sliced black olives. If the sauce seems to have dried out (which will happen if you've baked them for too long), add a little more before serving.

ANDREA

Max & Rosie's is my second family. When I worked at the café, I felt like the long-lost thirteenth cousin, separated at birth and twice removed. It was a perfect equation: A crew of Jews, plus a million smoothies, times a bunch of carrot juice, divided by Pure Synergy, equals the best job of my life.

Andrea, a University of North Carolina at Asheville student, came to Café Max & Rosie's looking for a summer job. As it turned out, we needed help on the juice bar at the time. We asked her to fill out an application. When we looked it over, we saw that her reference was none other than our wonderful rabbi! How could we do anything else but hire her immediately! She worked out great, and to this day we still consider her part of our family.

Max's Vegetarian Shepherd's Pie

SERVES 4 TO 6

Ladies, read no further. This is a guy thing. But if you must, you must. Let's be honest, guys, every man needs a recipe that is delicious and different. This one recipe will do more to make you a hero than months in the gym. Plus it's good fun. Let's get to it! (Oh, please note: This recipe is dishwashing-intensive.)

4 russet potatoes, peeled and chopped

4 tablespoons soy margarine

1 carrot, sliced

1 zucchini, sliced

1 to 2 tablespoons extra virgin olive oil

1 portobello mushroom, trimmed and cubed

1 (20-ounce) jar marinara sauce

1 cup cooked kidney beans, rinsed and drained (see page 11)

1 cup cooked garbanzo beans, rinsed and drained (see page 11)

Sea salt and freshly ground black pepper

Combine the potatoes with water to cover in a saucepan. Cover, bring to a boil, and simmer for 15 minutes, or until soft. Drain the potatoes, add the margarine, and mash. Set aside.

In a separate saucepan, steam the carrot and zucchini for 3 to 5 minutes, until the carrot brightens.

Heat the oil in a cast-iron skillet over high heat. Add the mushroom and sauté for 5 minutes, until soft. Lower the heat and add the sauce, beans, carrots, zucchini, salt, and pepper. Stir. Gently simmer, covered, for 5 to 10 minutes to allow the flavors to blend.

Transfer the bean and vegetable mixture into a 2 1/2-quart casserole dish. Top with the mashed potatoes and spread with a fork. Make beautiful designs. Place the dish under a broiler (preheat if using an electric oven) for 10 minutes to brown the top of the potatoes. Serve with a green salad.

Tofu Spinach Lasagne

SERVES 6 TO 8

Because lasagne is a food I didn't want to give up when I gave up cheese, I played with a vegan version for a while and this one stuck. It's popular in my house as well as at the café. Begin this recipe with the sauce, as the longer it cooks, the more flavorful it will be. If the filling isn't creamy enough, add a little more oil. I've served this to many people who had no idea it was made with tofu. Serve with salad and garlic bread. A meal no one could refuse!

Sauce

1 to 2 tablespoons extra virgin olive oil

2 ripe plum tomatoes, chopped

1 small onion, chopped

4 cloves garlic, minced

6 button mushrooms, trimmed and sliced

2 tablespoons dried oregano

1 tablespoon dried basil

3 (15-ounce) cans tomato sauce

1 (6-ounce) can tomato paste

Sea salt and freshly ground black pepper

12 lasagne noodles (about 12 ounces)

$1/2$ pound mozzarella-style soy cheese, grated

Filling

$1^{1}/2$ cups packed fresh or frozen chopped spinach

$1^{1}/2$ pounds firm tofu

$2/3$ cup freshly squeezed lemon juice

1 tablespoon honey

About $2/3$ cup canola oil

2 teaspoons sea salt

2 tablespoons granulated garlic

1 tablespoon dried oregano

Heat the olive oil in a heavy saucepan over high heat. Add the tomatoes, onion, garlic, and mushrooms and sauté for 5 minutes, until the onions are translucent. Lower the heat and add the oregano and basil. Stir. Then add the sauce and paste and stir until smooth. Bring to a slow boil and then simmer, covered, for at least 1 hour. Add salt and pepper and adjust seasonings.

While the sauce is simmering, cook the lasagne noodles in plenty of boiling salted water until al dente, about 10 minutes. Drain. Let the noodles sit in cold water until you are ready to use them. This will keep them from sticking.

Steam the spinach for 3 to 5 minutes, until bright green, and drain well.

Blend the tofu, lemon juice, honey, and canola oil in a food processor until smooth. Add the salt, granulated garlic, and oregano. Fold in the spinach. Adjust seasonings. This filling should have the consistency and taste of ricotta cheese.

Preheat the oven to 350°.

Cover the bottom of a 9 by 13-inch shallow baking dish with some of the sauce. Layer the noodles, sauce, and filling. (Each layer should have 4 noodles.) The top layer should be noodles, sauce, and grated cheese.

Bake, covered, for approximately 30 minutes. Uncover and bake for another 5 minutes.

Let stand for at least 10 minutes before serving.

Blackened Tofu Sandwich

SERVES 4

This is another very popular "daily special" at Max & Rosie's. Blackened dishes are known to be hot, depending on how much Cajun seasoning you use. So, unless you like hot foods, go easy. Remember, you can always add more if you want it spicier. Try this sandwich with tempeh as well. It's definitely one of my favorites.

1 pound firm tofu, sliced lengthwise into 4 pieces

1/2 cup tamari

Whole-wheat flour for breading

6 to 8 tablespoons canola oil

Cajun seasoning mix (you can buy this premixed)

8 slices whole-grain bread

Nayonnaise

4 leaves green lettuce

4 slices tomato

5 ounces alfalfa sprouts

Place the tofu on a plate and cover with the tamari. Turn the tofu until coated on both sides. Then dip it in the flour, turning once to cover both sides.

Heat the oil in a large cast-iron skillet until very hot. Sprinkle some Cajun seasoning into the oil and add the tofu. Fry for 5 minutes, until the bottom of the slice is black. (This doesn't mean to burn the tofu; it is the Cajun seasoning that turns it black.) Sprinkle more Cajun seasoning on top of the tofu, then turn it over and fry for 5 minutes more, until the second side is black.

Spread the Nayonnaise on the bread, then layer on the lettuce, tofu, tomato, and sprouts. Close the sandwich, cut in half, and serve.

Jericho Salsa

MAKES ABOUT 3 CUPS

Jericho, one of our newest employees, created this salsa and we loved it so much that now it is used exclusively at Café Max & Rosie's. It has become one of our select "top-secret" recipes. If it's too hot for you, reduce the amount of jalapeños. Muy Bueno!

¹/4 cup green bell pepper, chopped

¹/4 cup red onion, chopped

¹/4 cup packed chopped fresh cilantro

¹/4 cup sliced jalapeño peppers

2 cups tomatoes, diced

Juice of 1 lime

2 teaspoons extra virgin olive oil

5 teaspoons apple cider vinegar

Sea salt and freshly ground black pepper

Combine the bell pepper, onion, cilantro, and jalapeño peppers in a food processor or blender and purée. Place in a bowl with the tomatoes.

Add the lime juice, oil, and vinegar. Mix well and season with salt and pepper. Refrigerate before serving.

Menu

This is a great Italian dinner, and vegan to boot! It's another dinner that deserves guests and a nice bottle of Chianti. The soup is a variation of Creamy Corn Chowder. I would serve it in small bowls because the lasagne is filling. I make the garlic bread with olive oil and minced garlic (lots of garlic) and bake it, wrapped in foil, for 30 minutes at 350°.

Creamy Zucchini Soup / 70

Tofu Spinach Lasagne / 126

Garlic Bread

Mediterranean Salad / 86
with Ume-Balsamic Dressing / 97

Part II: Just Juice It!

An Introduction to
Max & Rosie's Juice Bar

Max & Rosie's juice bar began with a Champion juicer, a blender, carrot juice, and a smoothie of the day. It has grown quite a bit over the years. It now holds refrigerators, freezers, two commercial juicers, three Vita-Mix blenders, and offers close to forty freshly squeezed juices and smoothies. It's an integral part of Max & Rosie's, and we are now known as "the best juice bar in town."

We make all our juices to order, using only fresh fruits and vegetables. This is the most nutritious way to prepare fresh juices. Juice that sits will oxidize and lose a lot of its nutritional value. Fresh fruit and vegetable juices are excellent sources of vitamins, minerals, and enzymes. The green drinks, in particular, are loaded with chlorophyll, which is a great blood builder. Because juices demand very little of the digestive system, they are excellent for healing.

Aside from the many health benefits fresh juices have to offer, they can be quite tasty and refreshing, as most of ours are. Granted, there are some (especially a few of our tonic drinks) that may not delight the taste buds, but they delight the body in a healthful way.

Our fresh fruit smoothies are made with pure fruit juices and fresh or frozen fruit. The secret of a thick smoothie is not ice, as many of the juice bars use. It is freezing the fruit and then blending it with the juice. The more fruit, the thicker the smoothie. I know the more commercial smoothie shops use other ingredients, such as yogurt, milk, ice cream, honey, and smoothie mixes. We stick to all fruit and find them to be extremely tasty and thirst quenching, especially on hot summer days. But do make sure the fruit is ripe, or even overripe, to ensure the sweetness. We also offer nutritional powders to add to smoothies for that healthy buzz. These enhance the nutritional value of the drinks and, with the exception of spirulina, usually don't disturb the taste. Smoothies make for a great snack or a light, quick meal.

There are basically two main types of juicers—centrifugal and masticating. You only need one juicer, so choose based on personal preference. They both do the same thing, but are mechanically different. The centrifugal juicer chops the fruits or vegetables, spins them in a basket at high speed, and separates the juice from the pulp. The pulp remains in the basket until it is cleaned. I recommend the Acme Challenger for this type of juicer. A masticating juicer mashes fruit and vegetables and then squeezes the juice from the pulp through a screen. For this type of juicer I recommend the Champion.

You need a wheatgrass juicer only to juice wheatgrass. We use the original Wheateena Manual Juicer at Max & Rosie's. Even though you have to crank it yourself, we have found that this hand-cranked version extracts more juice from wheatgrass than the electric wheatgrass juicers.

And then, of course, there's the citrus juicer for oranges, grapefruits, lemons, and limes. We use a manual citrus juicer, which seems to work the best.

All of the juicers I've mentioned have stainless steel parts, which I highly recommend over plastic parts because they are better quality and longer lasting. Juicers can be found at most health food stores and some mail order companies.

"Just Juice It" gives you the ingredients of our juices and smoothies at Max & Rosie's Juice Bar. I hope you use them, enjoy them, and experiment with them; the possible combinations of fruits and vegetables are endless.

Class 10: Fresh Vegetable Juices

136

Part II:
Just Juice It!

Fresh
Vegetable
Juices

AN INTRODUCTION TO FRESH VEGETABLE JUICES

Although we try to use organic vegetables, we can't always get what we need. The one organic vegetable we use exclusively is carrots. The difference in flavor from commercially grown carrots is tremendous, so make every effort to find organic carrots in your juicing endeavors. Organic carrots are usually large, so be flexible with the measurements for these juices. All of the recipes will yield about 10 fluid ounces—1 serving.

Get to know which vegetables yield the most liquid. When making your own juice combinations, juice the high-liquid vegetables last; their liquid will move out the vegetables that need more liquid to juice.

If you feel a cold coming on, add fresh garlic juice or fresh ginger juice to any of the juices. For an extra healthy "buzz," add a shot of wheatgrass.

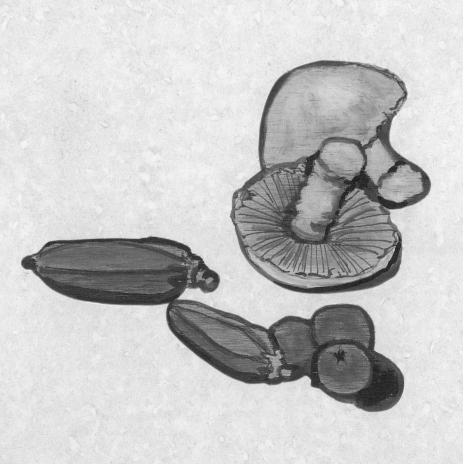

Gypsy Sunrise

SERVES 1

We call this juice our "CBC" (carrot, beet, celery). It's a tonic that could greet any sunrise.

1/4 beet

1 stalk celery

3 to 4 carrots, scrubbed

Juice the beet, then the celery, and finish with the carrots. Serve at once.

Garden Patch

SERVES 1

A great-tasting mixed vegetable juice. Great for rabbits, but even better for us!

1/4 beet

Handful parsley leaves

1 stalk celery

1/2 cucumber, peeled if not organic

2 to 3 carrots, scrubbed

Juice the beet, then the parsley, celery, and cucumber. Finish with the carrots. Serve at once.

Veggie Grass

SERVES 1

You can hear the "Juice Maiden" moan as this juice is ordered over and over again. The manual wheatgrass juicer requires quite the right arm muscle workout!

1/4 beet

Handful parsley leaves

1 stalk celery

3 to 4 carrots, scrubbed

1 ounce shot wheatgrass

Juice the beet, then the parsley and celery. Juice the carrots. Juice the wheatgrass in a wheatgrass juicer. Pour the vegetable juice into a glass and add the wheatgrass on top. Serve at once.

Cabbage Patch

SERVES 1

If those dolls got to drink some of this juice, they might not be so funny looking!

1/4 beet

1/4 head green cabbage

2 to 3 carrots, scrubbed

Juice the beet, cabbage, and then the carrots. Serve at once.

JENNIFER, AKA "THE JUICE MAIDEN"

I call them family, I call them friends...They've kept my belly full and given me the title "The Juice Maiden." It's like Sol told me, "Jennifer, you won't work here forever, it's just one of your many stops. But what you learn, take with you and use. Oh, and call your mother!"

Jennifer was a friend of Andrea's, and when Andrea returned to school, Jennifer replaced her on the juice bar. Initially, she was very shy, didn't talk much, and was Rosie's dream come true because she cleaned like no one before (except Marti, of course...). As time went on, Jennifer seemed to open up in many ways—her hair got shorter and shorter and went through a few colors, we noticed a little makeup now and then, and her whole body language began to change as she started *dancing* the food to the tables. She is now known as "The Juice Maiden" of Max & Rosie's, and rightly so. Even though she makes a great model (she's six feet tall and quite photogenic), we hope she stays with us for a long time to come.

Popeye

SERVES 1

I fight to the finish 'cause I drinks me spinach!

1 cup packed fresh spinach leaves

¹/₂ cucumber, peeled if not organic

3 to 4 carrots, scrubbed

Juice the spinach, cucumber, and then the carrots. Serve at once.

Elvis Parsley

SERVES 1

Had Elvis drunk his parsley, it would have cleaned his liver, kidneys,

and urinary tract. It might have stopped his blue suede shoes from wearing out!

Handful fresh parsley leaves

3 to 4 carrots, scrubbed

1 lemon, halved

Juice the parsley and the carrots and pour into a glass. Juice the lemon in a citrus juicer and add to the glass. Serve at once.

" The terrible punishment for living without attention is soft drinks, instant coffee, TV dinners, fast food places, and vegetables and fruits perfectly formed, tasteless, and lacking in nutrition. "

—Max

Sweet Heart

SERVES 1

This sweet and healthy juice will make any heart sweet.

- 1/2 beet
- 1 red apple
- 3 to 4 carrots, scrubbed

Juice the beet, apple, and then the carrots. Serve at once.

Orange Sunshine

SERVES 1

This juice will brighten any day. Its colors are quite psychedelic!

- 1 orange
- 3 to 4 carrots, scrubbed

Juice the orange in a citrus juicer and pour into a glass. Juice the carrots and add to the glass. Serve at once.

143

Class 10:
Vegetable Juices

Hawaiian Eye

SERVES 1

This is not a TV show, it's a juice chock-full of vitamin C and good for sore throats.

- 1/4 fresh pineapple
- 3 to 4 carrots, scrubbed

Juice the pineapple, then the carrots. Serve at once.

Class 11: Fresh Fruit Juices

Café Max & Rosie's

144

Part II:
Just Juice It!

Fresh Fruit
Juices

AN INTRODUCTION TO FRESH FRUIT JUICES

Our fresh fruit juices are a very popular alternative to our fresh fruit smoothies, as they are freshly squeezed to order and served over a small amount of ice, rather than blended. The mixtures of fruits are incredible tasting, and there are many more just waiting to be created. Again, depending on the size of the fruit, you may need more or less than these recipes call for. These recipes each make about 10 fluid ounces of juice to serve one.

Watermelon Patch

This juice is just watermelon juice, straight. I can tell you, in season, there is nothing more delicious. It is sweet and refreshing. You can juice the rinds, but as they are not sweet, it takes away from the sweetness of the watermelon. Make sure to watch out for the seeds when you're juicing—they fly everywhere!

1 1/2 cups cubed watermelon

Juice the watermelon. Serve at once over ice.

Purple Passion

SERVES 1

Picture a cluster of ripe, luscious grapes combined with a juicy red apple. With this image in mind you too will become purple with passion!

2 cups red grapes

1 to 2 red apples

Juice the grapes, then the apples. Serve at once over ice.

Apple Orchard

SERVES 1

This combination of apples, strawberries, and a little lemon creates a wonderful cleansing after that winter indoors.

3 to 4 fresh strawberries

1 1/2 to 2 red apples

1/2 lemon

Juice the strawberries and then the apples and pour into a glass. Juice the lemon in a citrus juicer and add to the glass. Serve at once over ice.

Strawberry Newton

SERVES 1

This combination of sweet fruits makes up for the lack of fig!

3 to 4 fresh strawberries

1/4 fresh pineapple

1 red apple

Juice the strawberries, then the pineapple, and finish with the apple. Serve at once over ice.

DANA

After deciding to study theatre in a program that would not be paying me a penny, I knew I had to find a job as soon as I finished school. So, in what I think was an attempt by my mom (Rosie) to get some female energy around the house, she suggested I live at home and work the juice bar at Max & Rosie's for the summer. I must say, you never know how hard something is until you do it. (And lemme tell ya, family does not get special treatment.) It's nothing-but-the-best service for the customers of Max & Rosie's. The boss makes sure of it. There is no question that I am not a natural like the rest of the family, but I did learn how to make a great smoothie in record time. (Well, maybe not record, but at least sufficient speed—right, Poppi?) I had a great time working at the café. Between the wacky staff and the quirky customers, every day was a new adventure. It's no mystery why people all over the world love and appreciate Café Max & Rosie's. It's a memorable experience.

Dana, Rosie's daughter, finished college and had three months before she took up her theatre internship in California. This is how she came to star at Café Max & Rosie's. Dana's frail beauty covered a very willful and determined young lady. Although she did not have the God-given talents of a juice maiden, she succeeded by will alone, and we were both very proud of the way she stuck it out, delighting all with her charming self. Her strong-willed character combined with her immense talent will surely take Dana to the top of her desired profession. Be sure to watch for her on Broadway!

Tropical Cooler

SERVES 1

For the heat of the summer nothing beats this tropical juice. It's very popular at Max & Rosie's.

1/4 fresh pineapple

1 cup cubed watermelon

1/2 lime

Juice the pineapple and then the watermelon and pour into a glass. Juice the lime in a citrus juicer and add to the glass. Serve at once over ice.

Ape Juice

SERVES 1

Let the monkey out and go ape with this delicious juice.

2 cups red grapes

1/4 fresh pineapple

1/2 lime

Juice the grapes and then the pineapple and pour into a glass. Juice the lime in a citrus juicer and add to the glass. Serve at once over ice.

Strawberry-Kiwi Cordial

SERVES 1

Not quite the same as those commercially bottled juices. This one is the real thing!

3 to 4 fresh strawberries

1 kiwi

1¹/₂ red apples

Juice the strawberries, then the kiwi, and finish with the apples. Serve at once over ice.

Class 12: Special Tonic Juices

Café Max & Rosie's

152

Part II:
Just Juice It!

Special Tonic Juices

AN INTRODUCTION TO SPECIAL TONIC JUICES

Our tonic juices are all formulated to do just what their names imply. If you have a hangover, we have a helper. Need energy? Have we got a juice for you. The mixtures of vegetables, sometimes with added supplements, seem to do the trick. They help to maximize health and boost the immune system. I would *like* to say these are deliciously refreshing. What I *can* say is they are wonderfully nutritious. So instead of reaching for the medicine cabinet next time you feel a cold coming on, try our 2-ounce shot of Cure the Cold!

All of the recipes (except Cure the Cold) are designed to yield about 10 fluid ounces or one serving.

Note: A few of these recipes call for a supplement called Pure Synergy. Pure Synergy is made from sixty of nature's most potent organic superfoods, and stimulates radiant health, mental clarity, immune system support, and energy. Contact the Synergy Company at 800-723-0277 or www.synergy-co.com for details.

Hangover Helper

Customers who order this usually say, "Not that I have a hangover!" We can always tell. So if not for you, give this juice as an act of charity to a friend. It works on the liver as well as clearing the head. Cheers!

4 lettuce leaves

1 cup dandelion greens

$1/2$ beet

2 carrots, scrubbed

1 ounce shot wheatgrass

Sprinkle cayenne pepper

Juice the lettuce, then the greens, then the beet, and finish with the carrots. Juice the wheatgrass in a wheatgrass juicer. Pour the vegetable juices into a glass, add the wheatgrass, and sprinkle the cayenne pepper on top. Serve at once.

Café Max & Rosie's

155

Class 12:
Tonic Juices

66 *It's time to begin cleaning up the planet.*

If we don't do it for us, how about for the children? 99

—*Rosie*

MASON

*I am the son of Rosie. I work at the café on
Saturdays. In the winter they call me Juice Man,
but in the busy season I get demoted to Dish Boy.
I don't mind; there's much less demand on dishes.
When you make juices you have to crank them out
so that people don't get them way after their food
has been taken to them. That's quite hard consid-
ering the rate at which the food is prepared.*

*I usually work with Poppi (my grandfather, aka
Sol) and Uncle Jeff (aka Chef Jeff). They're really
fun to work with. Poppi loves to make people
laugh. He's been in the food business for about
fifty years. He once told me, "The key to this business is making people feel comfortable. When
someone feels comfortable, then they think that*

the service was good, the food was good, and the price was good."

Uncle Jeff is really great to work with, too. He's very sociable and also likes to make people feel comfortable. Occasionally, when we are really busy, he does certain things to make us both laugh. Sometimes he tries to sing opera. That usually doesn't work out too well.

This has been my first real job. I don't think I'll be able to find another job that brings me as much joy as I have working at Café Max & Rosie's.

Mason started working at the café in the middle of winter. We figured it was slow enough then to try him out and see if he could do it. After all, he was only fifteen and had never worked before. Also, Mason has this trait that we call "going into Mason Land," or simply getting lost in his dreams on his way to doing something. We must say, however, he's worked out really well. Of course, working with his grandfather and uncle, he tends to get a lot of help, along with a bit of good-natured verbal abuse.

Blood Builder

SERVES 1

All strength needs to begin from the inside. This tonic is chock-full of chlorophyll and is great for building the blood. But watch out; it comes with a warning. It's also a potent detox for the liver.

    1 large beet

    1 cup fresh parsley

    1 cup alfalfa sprouts

    6 to 8 lettuce leaves, or more if needed to fill a 10-ounce glass

    1 ounce shot wheatgrass

Juice the beet, then the parsley, then the sprouts, and finish with the lettuce. Juice the wheatgrass in a wheatgrass juicer. Pour the vegetable juices into a glass and add the wheatgrass on top. Serve at once.

Sensational Skin

SERVES 1

It seems that only women order this one. Do the men think ordering it would make them seem too vain? Beautiful skin is a sign of good health, so drink up and watch for that healthy glow!

    Handful fresh parsley leaves

    1 cup fresh spinach leaves

    4 lettuce leaves

    1/2 cucumber, peeled if not organic

    2 carrots, scrubbed

    1 to 2 teaspoons Pure Synergy (see page 153)

Juice the parsley, then the spinach, then the lettuce, then the cucumber, and finish with the carrots. Pour the vegetable juice into a shaker container and add the Pure Synergy. Shake and serve.

Liver Lift

SERVES 1

Take good care of your liver. It's the only one you get!

1 cup fresh spinach leaves

1 cup fresh dandelion greens

1 beet

2 to 3 carrots, scrubbed

1 ounce shot wheatgrass

Juice the spinach, then the dandelion greens, then the beet, and finish with the carrots. Juice the wheatgrass in a wheatgrass juicer. Pour the vegetable juices into a glass and add the wheatgrass on top. Serve at once.

Cure the Cold

SERVES 1

How can so little do so much? This 2-ounce tonic is very warming and boosts the immune system. It is best to drink this when you are feeling the start of cold symptoms.

1 ounce (2 tablespoons) freshly squeezed lemon juice

^{3}/4 ounce (1^1/2 tablespoons) freshly squeezed ginger juice (see page 5)

20 drops (or more) echinacea tincture (available in health food stores)

Pinch cayenne pepper

Mix all the ingredients together and drink it down. You may want to follow it with some water.

Energy Enhancer

SERVES 1

There's nothing like cayenne to stimulate the liver, cleanse the blood, and put a sparkle in your eye. The addition of ginseng will have you dancing through your day.

> **2 cups fresh spinach leaves**
>
> **1 to 2 zucchini**
>
> **1 large tomato**
>
> **Ginseng powder or tincture (Available in health food stores. Follow label instructions for quantity.)**
>
> **Sprinkle cayenne pepper**

Juice the spinach, then the zucchini, and finish with the tomato. You may want to run $1/4$ cup of water through the juicer to get the remaining tomato juice. Pour the juice into a shaker container and add the ginseng. Shake gently and pour into a glass. Sprinkle the cayenne pepper on top. Serve at once.

Bye-Bye Blues

SERVES 1

Depression may well be a state of body. Bye-Bye Blues will brighten even the heaviest of days.

> **1 zucchini**
>
> **$1/4$ head green cabbage, cut**
>
> **$1/2$ cucumber, peeled if not organic**
>
> **2 carrots, scrubbed**
>
> **1 to 2 teaspoons Pure Synergy (see page 153)**

Juice the zucchini, then the cabbage, then the cucumber, and finish with the carrots. Pour the juice into a shaker container and add the Pure Synergy. Shake gently and pour into a glass. Get ready to feel better.

Class 13: Fresh Fruit Smoothies

Café Max & Rosie's

162

Part II:
Just Juice It!

Fresh Fruit Smoothies

AN INTRODUCTION TO FRESH FRUIT SMOOTHIES

We make our fresh fruit smoothies with fruit juice and frozen fruit, much of which we buy fresh and freeze ourselves. (Be sure to cut up the fruit before freezing.) We offer ten of them on our menu, but always let customers make up their own as well. We have seen some pretty interesting combinations develop over the years. Smoothies are our most popular drinks at the juice bar, especially in the summertime.

All of the recipes are designed to yield about 16 fluid ounces, or one serving. If this seems like a lot, don't worry. I guarantee you'll be wanting more!

All you need is a blender to get going. Make sure the frozen fruit is cut before blending and put the juice in first so as not to break the blades of the blender. Smoothies should be thick, but not so thick that you need to use a spoon. If your smoothie is not as thick as you'd like, add more fruit, as the size of fruits vary. I suggest you try some of our recipes and then begin blending your own favorite combinations. You can add any powdered or liquid supplements for a nutritious, low-fat snack or light meal. Just to let you know: smoothies can be addicting, in a good way of course.

Tahiti Sunrise

SERVES 1

This is probably our most popular smoothie at Café Max & Rosie's. It's simple, but get ready for the tropics!

1 1/2 cups orange juice

1/2 to 1 cup frozen whole strawberries

1 1/2 frozen bananas, cut in 8 pieces

Put all the ingredients in a blender, beginning with the juice. Blend to a desired consistency. Serve at once.

Georgia Peach

SERVES 1

This is the smoothie to put Georgia on your mind!

1 1/2 cups apple juice

1 cup frozen sliced peaches

1/2 cup frozen whole strawberries

Put all the ingredients in a blender, beginning with the juice. Blend to a desired consistency. Serve at once.

Apple Berry Forever

SERVES 1

This one is our son Joshua's favorite. A rare case where more equals better.

1^1/$_2$ cups apple juice

^{1}/$_2$ to 1 cup frozen blueberries

1^1/$_2$ frozen bananas, cut in 8 pieces

Put all the ingredients in a blender, beginning with the juice. Blend to a desired consistency. Serve at once.

Raspberratazz

SERVES 1

We have heard many hilarious attempts at pronouncing this one. We simply call it a "Razz." Don't worry about saying it; let the taste be enough.

1^1/$_2$ cups pineapple juice

^{1}/$_2$ to 1 cup frozen raspberries

1^1/$_2$ frozen bananas, cut in 8 pieces

Put all the ingredients in a blender, beginning with the juice. Blend to a desired consistency. Serve at once.

JERICHO

I've been working at Max & Rosie's on and off for about a year now. I've become extremely knowledgeable and more aware about my health while working there. The crew at Max & Rosie's has become my family in Asheville.

Recently, a rather serious young man joined our crew. He is, as we say in the food trade, a natural. He is clean and fast and really enjoys the fast pace of the food business. At times it can get a bit rocky on the personality level, but over time and mutual respect, our days are smoother and he has become a welcome new addition to the Max & Rosie's family. And as if that's not enough, he makes a great salsa!

Ring around the Rosie

SERVES 1

This is the All-American smoothie. We recommend you listen to the "Star Spangled Banner" as you drink it. God bless America.

> 1¹/2 cups apple juice
>
> 2 to 2¹/2 frozen bananas, cut in 16 pieces
>
> 1 heaping tablespoon freshly ground peanut butter

Put all the ingredients in a blender, beginning with the juice. Blend to a desired consistency. Serve at once.

It Takes Two to Mango

SERVES 1

Drink one with a friend and who knows? Are you ready to tango?

> 1 cup mango juice
>
> 1/2 cup apple juice
>
> Splash lime juice
>
> 2 cups seeded, cubed, and frozen watermelon

Put all the ingredients in a blender, beginning with the juices. Blend to a desired consistency. Serve at once.

Merry Berry

SERVES 1

This one is Rosie's favorite and seems to make her berry merry!

- 1 cup pineapple juice
- 1/2 cup coconut juice
- 1/2 cup frozen blueberries
- 1 cup frozen whole strawberries
- 1/2 cup frozen raspberries

Put all the ingredients in a blender, beginning with the juices. Blend to a desired consistency. Serve at once.

Razzmelon Cooler

SERVES 1

A refreshing smoothie favored by the regular customers of Max & Rosie's. It's cool, man.

- 1 cup coconut juice
- 1/2 cup pineapple juice
- Splash lime juice
- 2 cups seeded, cubed, and frozen watermelon
- 1 cup frozen raspberries

Put all the ingredients in a blender, beginning with the juices. Blend to a desired consistency. Serve at once.

Mango Strut

SERVES 1

This smoothie has been served many times with a strut in the walk. So if you're gonna strut your stuff, do it with mango!

- 1 cup mango juice
- $1/2$ cup apple juice
- 1 cup frozen sliced peaches
- 1 cup frozen whole strawberries

Put all the ingredients in a blender, beginning with the juices. Blend to a desired consistency. Serve at once.

One over the Eight

SERVES 1

In England, "one over the eight" means you've had one too many. So be drunk on this delightful, refreshing, and healthy smoothie!

- 1 cup papaya nectar
- $1/2$ cup coconut juice
- 1 cup frozen whole strawberries
- $1 1/2$ frozen bananas, cut in 8 pieces

Put all the ingredients in a blender, beginning with the juices. Blend to a desired consistency. Serve at once.

169

Class 13:
Fruit Smoothies

Epilogue

Not very long ago, there was a land rich and full of variety, a veritable symphony of beauty. This land was bountiful, and all who lived there ate well and had shelter.

Almost unnoticed, the people of this land began desiring more than they could ever use or need. Soon they had totally lost their way in stuff, losing their taste for quality. Quantity had become the thing. Before long there were people without food or shelter. People were consuming beyond their capacity, dying of heart disease, cancer, and even the tension of getting more stuff. The people felt powerless.

Then one day a few people of good will said, "No more. We are unhealthy in body and mind. There is another way to live." They were called eccentrics, vegetarians. Questions were asked. "How can you be healthy and happy with less?" The answer was loud and clear. "We are the evidence that a simple vegetarian lifestyle is healthier and more fulfilling than the path of saturated fats and animal products. Let's abandon quantity so that we do not run the risk of losing the quality of being human. This is an invitation to sanity."

All of the best stories have happy endings, and the best place to write the happy ending is right here. After all, journeys must begin from where you are. We have been blessed with the ability to correct our mistakes once we are aware of them. Fifteen years ago smoking was considered an acceptable habit; now the habit is strongly on the decline and has ceased to be socially acceptable. We will boldly predict that the next fifteen years will see new attitudes about the excessive consumption of animal products, about genetic engineering, and food irradiation. This new point of view will create a healthier, balanced, and more joyful planet. Choosing a healthy lifestyle changes everything.

May your journey be joyful.

Index

*Page numbers in italics indicate
menu suggestions.*